CAN THESE BONES
LIVE AGAIN?

Healing the Wounded Church

DON SHACKELFORD

WestBow
PRESS
A DIVISION OF THOMAS NELSON

WestBow Press books may be ordered through booksellers or by contacting:

WestBow Press
A Division of Thomas Nelson
1663 Liberty Drive
Bloomington, IN 47403
www.westbowpress.com
1 (866) 928-1240

ISBN: 978-1-4908-1631-9 (sc)
ISBN: 978-1-4908-1632-6 (hc)
ISBN: 978-1-4908-1630-2 (e)

Library of Congress Control Number: 2013921402

Printed in the United States of America.

WestBow Press rev. date: 11/20/2013

Contents

Jesus,
You are good, and Your mercy endures forever.
Let us love like You do.

Dedication

I dedicate this book to my wonderful wife, Brenda Mae Shackelford. Her love, encouragement, patience, understanding, support, and faith in me exceed my words. I can never say enough good about the "rib" God has blessed me with. When I found her, I found a good thing, and I have received the favor of God. Thank you for who you are and what you mean to me.

I love you!

Foreword

by Apostle Floyd Baker Sr.

For several years Don Shackelford has ministered to the fallen in a very effective and powerful jail ministry, even providing a home and work for those who wanted it. Don is one of the restored ones, and he is a man who has a passion for the lost and broken to be restored so they can be laborers in this last-days harvest.

For many years the church by and large has been terribly wrong in the way it has treated its fallen ones. We have wasted tremendously valuable and gifted resources. We have been burying them instead of restoring them according to the Scripture. Galatians 6:1 (KJV) says, "Brethren, if a man be overtaken in a fault, ye which are spiritual, restore such an one in the spirit of meekness; considering thyself, lest thou also be tempted. We have remembered discipline and forgotten that the command is to restore" (ref. Rom. 14).

In this book, Don Shackelford has brought to light our consciences and our responsibility. I have known Don for many years and have labored with him, and I can testify this book is not theory but well thought out and lived out on a daily basis. I challenge all Christians, all backslidden, and especially all pastors and elders to read this book even though it will challenge your thinking and traditions. After all, are we not almost all in agreement that our Lord Jesus will return soon for a "church without spot or wrinkle"?

—Apostle Floyd Baker, Sr.

Apostle Floyd Baker Sr. has been ministering for fifty-seven years. He traveled throughout the United States and many places in the world and conducted services where many medically documented miracles and healings took place. He was the evangelist for CBN's *700 Club,* working with Pat Robertson during the seventies. Since then he has traveled in many parts of the body of Christ ministering to pastors and churches.

Acknowledgments

This is a list of the men of God (in no specific order) who stood by my side during the darkest, driest, hardest days of my life. Without their love for the Lord and for me, this book would not have been possible.

- Sheriff Ray Nash
- Lt. Col. Mark Closson
- Pastor Cameron Kirker
- Pastor Seymour Cook
- Rev. Rick Lindsay
- Rabbi (Messianic) BJ Harris
- Tom Timm
- Bill Gadol
- Tom Epperson

I am forever indebted to you men for loving and believing in me when the world around me was closing in.

Endorsements

As a long-time friend and mentor, Pastor Don has a heart of compassion for those who have been hurt and wounded in the Army of God. He doesn't just speak about the hurt and wounded; he has personally traveled down that road and back many times. This book is Holy Spirit inspired, and has been written for such a time as this."
Pastor Steve Brunson, Mercy Heart Ministries

Some know the Bible, others do the Bible. A friend of many years I have watched Pastor Don walk out his faith. This is a true Man of God who not only knows the Word but does the Word every day. He has blessed me and my family time and time again and I know the experiences he shares in this book will bless you and yours as well. This is a man who I can trust with all that I have because I know he is owned by God and guided by the Holy Spirit.
William N. Gadol, President, FedMedical. Inc.

Pastor Don Shackelford has been my dear friend for over twenty years. We've ministered together in the US and in some of the most remote and dangerous places on earth. I have watched him handle all of the trials common to men, along with many unusual challenges that only pastors and missionaries seem to face. Additionally, Pastor Don has had personal health issues that were potentially life threatening and lost many close friends and family members to premature death. In every trial, Don has proven himself to be a true man of God and more than a conqueror. He is an overcomer in the Biblical sense of the word. Pastor Don shares from his own vast life experiences and points readers to his consistent trust in our Lord Jesus and the truth of God's Word. Enjoy and be blessed.

Pastor H. Pitts Evans, Pastor Whole Word Fellowship, Oakton, VA

It has been my privilege and joy to have worked very closely with Don for a number of years on some key projects. I found him to be a man of great passion and integrity. He has the uncanny ability to know when one mission is done and when it is time to start into the new one. I have watched both he and his precious wife Brenda lay everything on the line to give themselves to help others whether in the States or building a church or school in the War Torn Nation of Sierra Leone.

Apostle Floyd Baker, Sr.

Our US Special Forces intentionally deploy a seasoned well trained combat mission ready soldier behind enemy lines to function as Head Quarter's eyes and ears; and, to assist the Commander in Charge to determine the strengths or weakness of any potential enemy or threat. Wisely, In his book, "Can These Bones Live Again?", Pastor Don takes his reader into the fray of becoming a Forward Observer Team Member witnessing the remarkable spiritual battles that shake the resolve of the strong hearted and forge Kingdom Relationships into Faithful Allies of The Commander of All Commanders, The First and the Last, The Sustainer of All Things, The Keeper of Promise, The Dispatcher of Purpose; and known through the seen and unseen Kingdom Realms of Everlasting as "HIS MAJESTY" - - The King of Kings and The Lord of Lord's of all that is and all that is to come; i.e., THE LORD JESUS CHRIST! By drawing upon his battle tested experience, insight, and revelation knowledge from the study of God's Word, you will be drawn to embrace Don's motto: God is Faithful! This book is a fast read; however, you will read it a second and third time – It's GOOD STUFF!

Rev. Rick Lindsay, Founder/President of Encourage Men To Pray Ministries, Inc., Prayer Director of the National Coalition of Ministries to Men (NCMM) South Carolina State Coordinator for the National Day of Prayer Task Force

Pastor Don Shackelford is a black belt in spiritual warfare. Anyone seriously engaged in service to the King would do well to study his insights. I have witnessed firsthand Don's strong faith and inspirational grace when taking fire from the enemy. Allegorically speaking, if God issued a warrant for the devil, I would take Pastor Don and kick down the front gates of hell...!

Sheriff Ray Nash, ret.
President - Police Dynamics Institute, Inc.
Sr. VP (Training and Development) -
International Academy of Public Safety

The Wounded Army of God

Millions received Jesus as their Savior (or thought they did), lived for Him for a season, became wounded (often by other Christians), and fell away, never to be heard from or even to attend church again. Thousands of them entered into ministry with great excitement and a determination to conquer the world for their King, only to find themselves conquered by the world around them. They are down for the count, and many believe they are out forever.

Their wounds, disappointments, failures, offenses, and even fears are deep. They are so deep it seems they will never heal. Some of these injuries are so bad the wounded ones don't even want them to be healed. The injuries have become familiar to them and thus comfortable to live with. To be healed, forgiven, and restored would appear to cost the wounded more than they may be willing to spend.

These children of God feel hope has left them, and they fear to ever hope again. To believe they are even children of God has become a stretch for many of them. Their spiritual bones are dried up. Their hearts are broken and possibly hardened. Their souls ache, and their spirits have darkened.

But I have a question: *Can These Bones Live Again?*

Preface

A Shaking

There is a shaking among the prophets of God. Voices around the globe are beginning to proclaim the restoration of God's people. Soldiers of the cross who have been asleep in the hospitals of their wounded spirits are beginning to wake up. God is on the move, and warriors who belong in the army of the King of Kings—men and women who were once powerful in His ministry—are hearing the call to return to His service.

The true Church, the ones who are abandoning their own selfishness, pride, and egos, are being assembled as humble servants to aid in the rebuilding of the wounded. The word of the Lord is prophesying *life* and *breath* into the dried-up and scattered bones of the army of God.

Introduction

Revival Is Coming

Revival is coming, and it's coming fast. Time is short, and the clock is ticking. Revival is not the saving of new souls, as many of today's churches have tried to make it; that's called an awakening. Revival is the *re-viving* of souls that at one time were energized in the work of the Lord but have fallen asleep or been wounded too deeply to continue the fight. This revival will gather God's people from many areas, many races, and many denominations.

Every bone will come together under divine direction and find its proper place. Not a single person or gift will be missing. The divine providence and mighty power of God will build His Church, and every joint (person) will begin to supply nourishment and strength to the other joints (people) until we become *one* body.

God is sending His breath from the four winds from around the world to speak life back into these wounded warriors. They will stand up on their feet again, and they will be an exceedingly great army of the Lord. God will use them to cry out to lost souls for salvation as the Church prepares for the end-times gathering. The Church will know God has performed this work in spite of their religious doctrines, laws, and bylaws.

It is time for the Church to agree with the Spirit of humility, grace, and mercy. It is time for us to be the restorers of the fallen, the broken, and the shamed. It is time to join hands with the men and women whose lives have become a mess and encourage them to tell their message: the message of a restoring God; the message of a forgiving God; and the message of how God picked them up out of the ashes, out of the dung, and out of the poor choices they made and set them back up on their feet.

It is time to become the revival!

My Story; Why This Message Is Important to Me

I've Fallen And I Can't Get Up!

There I was, minding my own business, enjoying a life of ministry. The Lord instructed me to encourage men in the South Carolina Lowcountry to become involved in a ministry movement teaching men to become men of integrity called Promise Keepers. My dear friend Ray was the owner and trainer of an area martial arts studio. When we discussed this movement, Ray decided (excitedly) to open his dojo and offer eight weeks of informal instruction and information to the men of his martial arts classes on how to become men of integrity based on the Promise Keepers seven promises model.

All of a sudden, this eight-week, informal, instructional training took on a life that could only come from the Spirit of God. Now known as the "Eight-Week Series," classes began to open up around the entire Lowcountry. The Lord was introducing me to pastors from every denomination, and most of them agreed to teach a class based on one (or more) of the seven principles of the

Promise Keepers model. A meeting was scheduled every day of the week, and hundreds of men were now learning these seven principles. Lives were changing, broken homes were being restored, and the glory of God was moving in a powerful way.

Then it happened. The Enemy became scared, and his anger was hot. He became busy sowing discord among the very men who were being raised up to be leaders in this incredible move. The spirit of jealousy started to rise, and men started to jockey for position. The spirit of anger stepped in, and before we knew it, an implosion was about to occur. False accusations were levied against me. I was told to leave the church or I would be destroyed. I was devastated. Obviously I had become a failure in the very midst of teaching others to become men of integrity. Now the spirit of confusion was running rampant in my heart. I was doing everything possible to help other men rebuild their lives, and mine was falling apart.

My accusers were angry beyond description, and I was confused beyond description. Before I knew what had happened, there was an attempt to end my life and my ministry and destroy my name. I was subsequently arrested and charged with a crime I did not commit, and I spent the next two years proving my innocence. The ministry of teaching men to become men of integrity and build strong families, churches, and communities was ended. I was publicly shamed, immediately homeless, and most of all, hopeless beyond description. In the midst of ministry, busy about the Father's business and building in the kingdom of God, all of a sudden I was down for the count.

Down for the Count!

Where did I go wrong? What did I do that caused me to fall so hard, so fast, and so far? I went from being an admired leader in the community to being a disgrace to the King of Kings in the twinkling of an eye. What sin did I commit? What crossroads was I at when I took the wrong turn? What decision did I make that brought me here? By that time (1994), I had been teaching about the grace of God, His enduring mercy, and the hope He gives to all those who trust in Him for the biggest part of twenty-six years. Now life was so bad I questioned if God—the God I had believed in, the God I had taught, the God I had loved, the God I had served from the age of sixteen—was even real. I cannot begin to describe my state of confusion at that time.

Meanwhile, God was busy telling me to share with anyone who would give me an audience that He was a faithful God! *Are you kidding me?* How would I ever be able to say that? He did not look faithful, and He did not feel faithful. In fact, faithful was the last thing He appeared to be to me. I was laying there wounded and spiritually bleeding beyond description while working with all my heart for my King He allowed lies, false accusations, deception, and the turning away of my friends, my coministers, men I was raising up in the ministry, and even family members. Now I was supposed to tell the world He was faithful? Really? Really? *Really*?

I know what it is like to fail. I know what it is like to be confused in life. I know what it is like to have your friends turn against you. I know what it is like to have your family mad at you. I know what it is like to be falsely accused, misunderstood, and rejected. I know what it is like to be homeless, unemployable, and living without hope while you wonder where your next meal will come from. I know despair. But I also know what it is like to be in school with God during these times. I know what it is like to learn a true life lesson in the class of hard knocks and bangs, and I know what it takes to get back up and keep going. I know how to find the light at the end of your tunnel. I know the true restoration of God through the power of the blood of His Son and the strength of His Holy Spirit during these impossible situations and difficult days. I know God, and He knows me. He knows my name.

He Knows My Name

I cannot express enough how the confusion was without description. I was hurting on a brand new level—a level I didn't even know existed. I was praying to a God that now seemed so far way He probably didn't even exist.

Everything I had believed in for twenty-six years seemed to vanish in an instant.

All hope, all peace, and all expectation of a creating and loving God was gone, and I was left standing alone. I decided to utter one last prayer. I dug down deep inside of everything God had deposited in me over the past twenty-six years. Everything I learned, everything I believed, and everything I had taught about this loving and merciful God and the prayer came out. I said to the Lord, "I need You to bless me. I don't even know if You exist right now, but if You do, then I need you to bless me. I don't know how that looks, but if You exist, then do something to bless me, *please* ..."

On Friday mornings, the pastor of the local PCA church would open the doors of his church around 5:30 a.m., set up one or two tables lengthwise, and invite the men of his congregation and the community to join him for a short devotional and time of prayer. At the time, I had been attending those Friday-morning meetings for about a year and a half. On an average Friday morning three to five men would show up and fellowship over a short devotional and time of prayer. On a good Friday morning, there could be as many as eight of us show up for this fellowship.

This Friday morning was different. I arrived earlier than the other men. I was in that emotional place that God had to show me something or I would just curl up and take my last breath. Life was barely worth living. When I entered the sanctuary, something was different. Instead of one or two tables lined up, there were a number of tables set up in a U-shape, and the pastor was sitting in the open end of the U. He was somewhat strange that morning, and I wasn't sure what to think.

Then the men started to come through the door. At first there were two, then three, then five, then eight, and within a few minutes, there were nineteen men in that room sitting around those tables ready for the morning devotional and prayer time. The pastor stood up and announced to all of us that he had not slept at all during the night. Instead, he had passed the night praying for all of us in that room. In his long night prayer, he specifically asked the Lord to wake up each and every one of us and bring us to that meeting, and the Lord answered his prayer. He then announced what he was about to do next was as far outside of his comfort zone and theology as he could ever remember. The Lord had given him specific instructions, and he was going to follow them even though he did not understand why it was necessary.

The pastor then said, "I have to lay hands on each of you and pray a blessing over you ..." I was done! Put a fork in me and turn me over, done! The Lord had just answered my prayer in His exceedingly, abundantly, and above all we can ask or think manner He is known for. He not only gave me a blessing, but He also gave nineteen other men (including the pastor) the same blessing! The men in that room were trying to console me because I was a blubbering piece of clay. I could hardly stand on my own two feet and was unable to explain to them what had just happened. Everyone thought I was done at that moment. What they failed to realize was the fact that I was just about to get started.

God revealed Himself to me in a way I never expected. He had just answered me nineteen times over, and now no demon in hell would ever be able to whisper in my ear the possibility of God not existing. Now I knew, not only does He exist, but He also takes personal pride in me as His own son. He knows my hurts, He understands my confusions, He feels my pains, and He knows me by my name! When I have a flaw or when I fail Him or fall short of His glory, He is not willing to throw me aside as unworthy, but instead, He is willing to hold me in His hands and mold me better into His image and finally "make me again another."

God brought twenty of His men who had His mind into one room to prove to me the power and influence of heaven we have when we are *one*.

Made Me Again Another

The day came for me to attend my first civil court hearing. It was one hearing of many to come. The Lord had given me specific instructions not to obtain a lawyer. The Lord said He would be my defense. I had no problem trusting what He told me now. I knew He existed, I knew He loved me, and I knew He knew the truth.

I was attending the local PCA church. The pastor was a man after God's heart and he was my friend, but he did not know if I was guilty or innocent of the charges against me. I shared with him what the Lord told me about being my defense and not to hire a lawyer. Then I thought it would be wisdom to share the defense strategy I had put together for court. After quietly listening to my strategy, the pastor looked at me and said, "I thought you said the Lord told you He would be your defense?"

I excitedly responded, "He did; that's why I put this together."

The pastor then shocked me with a challenge I never saw coming. He said, "Well if the Lord is going to be your defense, then you don't need to say anything!" He reminded me, even though he was my pastor and friend and wanted to believe me, he really didn't know the truth, and it looked like I could be guilty.

Shocked and in disbelief, I wanted to verify my understanding of what my pastor was asking me to do or in this case, not to do. So I asked him, "Are you saying I should go to court and say nothing in my defense at all?"

He responded, "Well, yes. It may be the only way we will ever know the truth."

I told him that was a pretty big pill to swallow, and after I flooded the sanctuary with my tears, I agreed to do just that—go to court, say absolutely nothing in my defense, and suffer whatever consequences the judge saw necessary to punish me with. God would be my defense, and He would either allow me to go to jail or exonerate me. Then my pastor proceeded to tell me he didn't know how he would respond if the tables were turned and I was asking him to do the same thing. That didn't exactly make me feel very comfortable, but I was going to follow through with my silence anyway.

We went to court, and the proceedings began. My best friend Ray was allowed to sit beside me in court. My pastor was allowed to sit behind us and observe the hearing. The accusing lawyer stood up to tell the account of the crime I was being charged with. I sat there in silent agony, waiting for the gavel to fall and praying I would be able to endure whatever would happen next.

When the accusing attorney finished and sat down, the judge looked at me with great disdain and what appeared to be great anger. He asked me, "Young man, do you have anything to say for yourself?"

I looked to my left at Ray and then behind me at my wondering pastor, turned to face the judge, and said, "No sir, Your Honor, I have nothing to say …"

All of a sudden, my accuser was infuriated. Standing up, and against the attorney's counsel, my accuser said, "If he has nothing to say, then I want to say something."

The judge said, "Go ahead," and then my accuser began to tell my side of the story … I walked out of court as free as a bird! Asking both Ray and my pastor what had just happened, my pastor responded, "The Lord just showed us you were innocent."

Now it was time for me to begin the process of renewing my strength while waiting upon the Lord.

No Strength Left

God, my defense, exonerated me of the false charges reported against me in the eyes of my dearest friend Ray and our pastor. However, as far as the system was concerned, there were many more trials I would face before I was legally released from these charges. For the next two years, I would face civil judges and criminal judges and lawyers from my accuser. If that wasn't enough, many people, including friends from other states, family members, neighbors, and members in the church I attended, had their opinions about who I was and what I was guilty of. The truth wasn't important to most of them. The accusation was all they needed to form their opinion and pass their judgments against me.

It was during this time in life I discovered America's biggest lie: "a person is innocent until proven guilty …" I quickly discovered the nature of the human race is to believe the negative accusations leveled against their fellow man until he proves himself innocent. Even then, many reserve the right to accuse, reject, and otherwise help destroy the one who has been charged, regardless of his innocence.

I understood how Job must have felt. Still despised, rejected, and judged as guilty by my fellow man, life continued to bring me confusion, hurt, anguish, and a host of other emotions, too many to list in this writing. Every morning I would get up and just try to get through the day. I would work at whatever my hands could find to do and make sure I worked enough hours that falling asleep wouldn't be a problem because exhaustion would just take over. I had no place to call home, but the Lord provided a place for me to lay my head down and rest every night. Sometimes I would sleep on a friend's couch. Sometimes I would be provided a bed in various homes of various friends, and sometimes I would sleep in a business office, but I was never without a place to sleep.

During these days the pains inside of me cannot begin to be described. I became emotionally, physically, financially, mentally, and spiritually exhausted. I was at my wit's end! It seemed as though I was nothing more than a dead man walking around trying to find his grave and often wishing it would all just come to an end. I was busy waiting for God do something only He could do. I needed my strength renewed, and I had no ability to renew it. If I was to survive then I needed to be restored.

Restore Such a One

"Brothers, if a man be overtaken in a fault, restore such a one ..." These words resounded in my ears at a new level. I was the one who was a failure in marriage. I was the one who had fallen. I was the one who needed someone, many someones, to come along beside me and pick me up.

In my case, the church overall failed in the command to "restore such a one." The pastors I had built relationships with were the first ones to turn me away. Some of them gathered together at the beginning of the implosion, called me into a meeting, looked me in the eyes, and informed me that I would leave the ministry the Lord had me start or they would "destroy it themselves." Talk about being devastated!

God sent a few men to stand with me, a few men who still cared enough to help me. There were men who remained my friends even though they were not sure of my guilt or innocence. There were some who decided to help me because it was the right thing to do. There were others the Lord forced to help me, in spite of their religious and judgmental hearts. New relationships were being formed, and God saw to it that I was cared for. He began to restore me Himself.

I asked the Lord what He wanted me to learn from all of this. He responded, "I want you to learn My majesty."

The answer stunned me, and I quickly replied, "Lord, how is that possible? You are too much for a man to learn such a thing."

He said, "Study My size, study My love, and study who I am ..."

With that conversation, I began to flail around the Scriptures, trying to be obedient to what the Lord told me, only to find myself even more confused and really not knowing how to accomplish such a huge study.

One afternoon at lunch, while washing my hands in the restroom, the Lord spoke to me and said, "Memorize My names." I chuckled and thought that would be tough. I already knew there were over seven hundred names of God listed in the Scriptures. Upon drying my hands and meeting my friend Rick at our table, I repeated my conversation with the Lord to him. I expected Rick to tell me that would be difficult at best and that I was probably just imagining such a conversation anyway. But I was wrong. Rick said, "Well, I have the list of God's names in my truck. I'll go out and get them for you!" Now who carries a list of God's names in their truck these days? Little did I know at that time, to understand the names of God, one would gain an understanding of the majesty of God!

It was time for me to rise up as a man of God and learn who my God really is! God Himself was about to restore me.

Deep Wounds

My wounds were deep and my pain was intense, but it was in these wounds and because of my personal pains I was forced to find promises from God that would sustain me until He would restore me. I needed to remember what His Word had said to me over the years. I was forced to dig deep inside of my heart and attach His promises, like an anchor, to the very core of my being. Here are some of those promises I clung to with all my heart and refused to let go, no matter how bad things were.

1) "Lo, I am with you always, *even* unto the end of the world" (Matt. 28:20).
2) "I will never leave you nor forsake you" (Heb. 13:5).
3) "What he promises He is able to perform" (Rom. 4:21).

4) "For I know the plans I have for you says the Lord. Plans to prosper you and not to harm you, plans for hope and a future" (Jer. 29:11).

5) "For with God nothing shall be impossible" (Luke 1:37).

6) "For thou hast made the heavens by thy great power ... nothing is too hard for thee" (Jer. 32:17).

7) "Now unto Him that is able to do exceedingly abundantly above all we ask or think according to the power that is at work within us" (Eph. 3:20).

8) "We are blessed us with all spiritual blessings in heavenly *places* in Christ" (Eph. 1:3).

9) "We are made holy without blame before him in love" (Eph. 1:4).

10) We are adopted by the king of the universe" (Eph. 1:5).

11) "We are made accepted in the beloved" (Eph. 1:6).

12) "We are redeemed through his blood" (Eph. 1:7).

13) "He lavished us with all wisdom and understanding" (Eph. 1:8).

14) "He opened to us the mystery of his will" (Eph. 1:9).

15) "He gave us an inheritance in his predestined purpose" (Eph. 1:11).

16) "He sealed us with the holy spirit of promise" (Eph. 1:13).

17) "He quickened us *[made us alive]* together with Christ" (Eph. 2:5).

18) "He put us together and made us sit together in heavenly places" (Eph. 2:6).

I soon realized trouble can be a blessing because you cannot have victory without a conflict, and you cannot win the battle if you never have a battle. You will never know He is the provider if you never have a need, and you will never know He is the healer if you are never sick. You will never know He will move a mountain if you never had a mountain in your way, and you would never know the power of God if you never have an affliction for Him to prove His power over.

Before I was wounded so deeply, these were nice promises. Now, in the midst of my wounds, I found healing in these promises. They became *my* promises and *my* anchor for *my* soul because there is life in our wounds.

It is good for me that I have been afflicted;
that I might learn thy statutes. (Ps. 119:71)

Rise Up, oh Man of God

When I was at my wit's end, the Lord instructed me to make a phone call to a man in Texas I had never met but I had heard of his testimony. He was a very wealthy man with an incredible testimony of how the Lord was using him in the land of Israel. I thought there was no way this man would receive a phone call from a stranger in South

Carolina who was a big mess in every aspect of his life, but I would try anyway. When the phone rang, *he* picked it up. I was amazed but sure by now I indeed had heard the Lord instruct me to make that call.

I shared my distressed life story with this stranger and wondered why he didn't hang up on me. This stranger in Texas took me to Psalm 107:23–31, where I found courage to stand back up on my feet and rejoin the army of God. While I was busy in the Father's kingdom, "doing business in great waters, the Lord commanded a stormy wind to raise me up on its waves and drop me down again to the depths. My soul was truly melted because of all of my troubles. I was going around and around and staggering like a drunken man, and I had reached my wit's end. Now in the midst of my trouble, I was crying out to the Lord, and I had the assurance He was about to bring me out of my distresses, calm my storm, and bring me to my desired haven …"

From that point on, I was willing to engage in life again. Soon following that encounter I was challenged to intentionally get up every morning at 2:00 a.m., go outside, and pray from two to three. Since there was a church near the business I was sleeping in, I decided to walk to the church and pray for the pastor, his ministries, and whatever else they might be involved in. I didn't know anyone in that congregation, and I wasn't aware of any specific needs they might have, so I just prayed for them.

Sometimes I would lay at the front door of that church as the Holy Spirit would come over me and find myself in great agony over the happenings there. I was interceding for them for reasons I was unaware of.

Three years passed since the day of my implosion. It was Sunday afternoon in November of 1997. I was now living in my own trailer, and things started to turn around for me. I had work every week, and I was sharing a new name of God every Sunday with the PCA church. The pastor would allow me two to three minutes each week to help inspire the people of his congregation. I was passionate about the things God was showing me of His Majesty, and that passion seemed to be contagious. The people were enjoying what they were learning. We were falling in love with each other and in love with God more and more every week. After service on that particular Sunday afternoon, the Lord told me to go to the church and pray at 2:00 p.m. Pieces of a grand-sized puzzle were about to come together and produce a beautiful picture.

For two years my prayers were under the cover of night. No person on the earth was aware of what was happening at 2:00 a.m. concerning the church. It was a secret closet, and it was only between the Lord and me.

That afternoon, obeying the Lord, I went to pray twelve hours early. Sure enough, I was caught red handed by the man who hired me to do odd jobs every week. Gary couldn't understand why I was busy praying at a church that was not the one I regularly attended.

Two weeks later, while I was painting the living room walls in one of Gary's rental units, there was a man working on the stove in the kitchen. The area between us was open, and we started a general conversation that led to attending church. The question arose about what church the appliance man attended, and he responded, "Flowertown Baptist Church on Boone Hill Road."

Gary was down the hall painting the bedroom. He was listening to our conversation and decided to speak up. Gary said, "Hey, Don, that's the church I caught you praying at!"

Bill, the appliance man, stopped working, turned toward me, and asked, "What is he talking about?"

I responded, "Oh, I was walking around the parking lot the other day praying for your church, and Gary drove by and saw me."

Bill asked me, "Why would you be praying over our church?"

Now my secret was no longer a secret, and I wasn't sure if Bill was confused or angry with me. "Well, the Lord impressed on me to pray for your pastor and ministries, so I was just being obedient."

"How long have you been doing that?" Bill asked.

"About two years," was the response. Bill asked for my phone number and contact information.

A few days passed, and my phone rang with a number I didn't recognize. When I answered the unknown phone call, there was a gruff-sounding voice on the other end that said, "I want to meet you ..." Confused and a little concerned I agreed to meet with Harry, the gruff voice. Harry gave me directions to his house, so I reluctantly ventured over to meet with him and had no clue what our meeting would entail. After I knocked on Harry's door, he opened it and said to me, "The kitchen is over there. Have a seat."

I wasn't sure if it was safe to go in or if I should run the other way. Harry failed to even say hello. He just went right to directing me to his kitchen table. I wasn't sure if we were about to eat or if he was about to eat me! Once we were sitting at the table, Harry, a very elderly man, pulled his chair up, looked me in the eyes, and said, "I can't afford a full-time preacher!"

Flabbergasted and really confused, I responded, "I didn't know I was putting in an application!"

"You have been praying over my church, haven't you?"

Since our conversations were so limited and I was caught in a world of not knowing who this man was or why he had even called me in the first place, I responded, "Well, I don't know. What church are you talking about?"

"Flowertown Baptist Church" he said.

"Yes, I have been praying over your church."

"How long have you been doing that?"

"About two years," was my reply.

"What are you praying for?"

"Well, I've been praying for you and your ministries, I guess."

"Why would you do that?" Harry asked.

"The Lord told me to. He put your church on my heart, so I have been interceding for you."

Harry looked into my eyes as though he was attempting to see into the depths of my soul, and then he said, "I'm tired, and I don't know how much longer I can keep going. For the past two years I have been asking the Lord to show me who He wanted to be my replacement!"

If I had not endured the implosion three years prior, if I had not been sleeping in the business next door, if I had not been studying the names of God and learning His majesty, if I had not allowed the Lord Himself to defend me and begin to restore me, if I had not taken the challenge to pray every night at 2:00 a.m., and if I had not obeyed the command to pray twelve hours early on a Sunday afternoon, I would not have been standing on this precipice now. I was about to reengage in the ministry of my King at a higher level. I was about to run to the battle for souls as the pastor of Flowertown Baptist Church.

The Battle Is the Lord's

I spent three years in school with the Lord. I wouldn't trade those three miserable, terrible, wonderful, marvelous years for anything the world has to offer me. The Lord taught me so many things and proved so many other things to me during those years, and they have become the most precious years of my life. One of the greatest lessons I now have as my very own truth that no man, no demon, and no circumstance can ever take from me is the fact that I belong to the Lord and He belongs to me.

I am His son, and He is my Savior, my Friend, my Lord, the Lover of my soul, my King, my Provider, my Supply, my Defense, my High Tower, my Rock, my All in All, my Hope, my Strength, my Righteousness, my Vine, my Bread, my Light, my Righteous Judge, my Redeemer, my Advocate, my Shepherd who leads me through dark places, my Faith, my Peace, my Deliverer, my Life, my Healer, my Great Physician, my Sure Foundation, and my Amen and Amen. Life will not end until He is finished with me. He is not only my King, but He is also the King of the universe. He is not only my Lord, but He is also the Lord of All. The world is His, I am His, the gold and silver are His, and the souls of all men are His. The heart of all the judges are in His hands, and the courts will do what He says.

I learned that when I fail Him, He never fails me. In fact He rejoices over me with singing, and when I turn my eyes toward Him, His heart is ravished with love for me. I learned when He is for me, it just doesn't matter who tries to be against me. My enemies are powerless, and my Friend is all powerful. I learned that I can hide myself under the shadow of His wings, and when I need to rest from the troubles of the world, He stands guard over me and commands His host of heaven to protect me. I have learned firsthand that no weapon formed against me will prosper and the lying tongues that rise up against me will be condemned by me because my Daddy, the King of Kings, has included this power and this right in my inheritance package.

Restoring What the Locusts Have Eaten

An important part of my life is contained in the restoration work of the Lord—work that only He could do and has done. Without knowing He restored me, why would someone even care about what I have written in these pages?

In my broken state of being, I lost family, friends, ministry, and all semblance of a good life. My wife was gone, my children didn't have time for me, other family members were just not sure who I was or what I did or didn't do, and all of those relationships were affected in some negative way. My friends were not much different, and the confusion they all had was a major strain on all of my friendships.

All of the ministry efforts I worked in and with were totally gone, and most of the ministers who knew me would shy away when I entered the room. I was homeless, unemployable and without hope of any kind. I spent two years proving my innocence and seven years living alone, without a human companion. But God was not finished with me yet.

After the first two years, I began to receive appointments to preach at churches I had never heard of, and the Lord provided a mobile home for me to live in as well as enough work to pay for the monthly rent and utilities. After the third year, He handed me Flowertown Baptist Church to pastor, and I have been the longest-standing senior pastor in the history of that church now for the past fifteen years.

Twelve years ago (after seven years of being alone), the Lord presented me with my soul mate, Brenda Payne LaTampa, who had suffered the loss of her husband of twenty-two years on Christmas Eve to a fatal heart attack. I argued with Him about not being interested in another woman until He made me take a good long look at this beautiful creature He was presenting to me. Today, twelve years later, we are still on our honeymoon. Upon our union in holy matrimony, Brenda assumed the lead role in the childcare facility I founded at the church.

Together, Brenda and I founded a private Christian school, a men's drug and alcohol recovery ministry, and a safe house for abused women and children. As the chief chaplain for twelve years at our county jail, we successfully established regular church services and Bible studies for the incarcerated men and women. I personally witnessed hundreds of men and women give their hearts to the Lord, and many remain in His service today.

Three years after marrying Brenda, the love of my life, she led a seven-member team of missionaries, including two teenagers and five mothers, to Mozambique, South Africa, to open a sixty-five-bed orphanage that has become the model orphanage in Mozambique.

Currently we are spending time on the mission field in Sierra Leone, West Africa, building churches, private Christian schools, and agriculture projects in the forgotten villages of the country. The vision we received from the Lord was to have a school in every village. Our immediate plans in Sierra Leone include the addition of new industries in the villages as a means of changing their financial infrastructure.

My children have all been reconciled to me, but more importantly, they have all been reconciled to the Lord and are serving Him. We just came home from meeting our twenty-fourth grandchild. In a few days we will welcome our twenty-fifth grandchild to our family, and in seven months we will welcome number twenty-six. Our kids are not done having children of their own, and we watch with great joy as the Lord continues to add to our posterity in great numbers.

I have a good life now. Everything and everyone the Enemy took from me has been restored to me over and over and over and over and over and over and over again. We continue to reach souls for the Lord in the United States and abroad. When I stood up to the Enemy, took my rightful place in the kingdom of God, held the line, and refused to die without one more try, God moved in and the Enemy had to get back under my feet.

Chapter 1

Smoking Flax

The Story of Soul

There once was a man named Soul who was walking in a garden. He was whistling a sweet tune for he was saved and had the joy of the Lord, but he was a baby Christian. As Soul was walking, a beautiful and seductive woman came out from behind a tree. Soul was very startled. He said, "Hello, I'm Soul. What is your name?"

She replied "I am Temptation. I have what you want."

"What do I want?" replied Soul.

"You want to do all things that are of the flesh," said Temptation.

Soul replied, "Okay, lead me." So he and Temptation went off and fulfilled the desires of the flesh.

When Soul returned to the garden, he met a man named Condemnation. Condemnation said, "Hey, I see you have met my friend, Temptation."

Soul said, "Yes, who are you?"

"I am Condemnation. I come after Temptation. We work hand-in-hand." Then Condemnation jumped on Soul's back and began to beat him. He hit him in the face and kicked him when he was down. This went on for a few days.

On about the third day, a man named Mercy came running up and said, "I command you, Condemnation, to stop beating Soul."

Condemnation snickered. "Make me."

So Mercy unsheathed his sword and cut Condemnation in two. As Soul watched in astonished pain, he was overtaken by the power of Mercy. Mercy walked up to Soul and said, "I have dealt with Condemnation before. He should not show up around you anymore."

Soul replied, "How can I ever thank you?"

"Well," replied Mercy, "God sent me here, and He told me to introduce you to a dear friend of mine. His name is Redemption."

Redemption walked up and said, "Hello, Soul. I see that you are not doing well."

Soul replied, "Not until Mercy came along. It is a pleasure to meet you, Redemption."

"Well," said Redemption, "I am glad to meet you. Are you ready to accept me?"

"What do you mean?" asked Soul.

Redemption said, "Well, when you accepted Jesus and decided to walk with Him, you chose to accept the things of Him and His love. I am a part of Jesus' love. I help you feel forgiven. You will never have to deal with Condemnation again. Temptation may come around, but I have someone I would like for you to meet who can help you with that. His name is Grace."

Grace walked up to Soul and said, "Hello, Soul. I have been waiting for you. As a matter of fact, all three of us have been waiting to meet you. I will help you take the way out of Temptation that God gives you as it comes up. The last person we want you to meet is Faith."

"Hi, Soul, I am Faith, and I will help you stay strong and keep your beliefs strong," said Faith.

Soul began to cry. When he began to cry Redemption said, "This is what we were here for. Jesus redeemed you, saved you by Grace through Faith and gives you His Mercy. Jesus loves you, Soul."

Soul said, "I love You, Jesus. God bless you *all!*"

(Author Unknown)

Bruised By Life

> A bruised reed shall he not break, and the smoking flax shall he not quench: he shall bring forth judgment unto truth. (Isa. 42:3)

> A bruised reed shall he not break, and smoking flax shall he not quench, till he send forth judgment unto victory. (Matt. 12:20)

We always judge others by their faults and failures instead of their successes. People of God may be successful in ministry for many years, but then one day they are discovered to have a secret sin they have hidden from the world. All of a sudden the work they have labored to accomplish is forgotten, and they are labeled as fallen or a failure. Be sure the Lord will not allow hidden sin to stay hidden forever, for our sin will find us out, and sin needs to be repented of.

Hidden sin is revealed so the world will know God governs the universe in truth and justice. It is His way of correcting His children as their heavenly Father and likewise warning wicked men they will be without excuse concerning their sins on judgment day. However, since we have all fallen short of God's glory, it would behoove us to discover the best way to restore a fallen soldier of the cross instead of trying to fire another shot of judgment into him or her. The Lord tells us to restore the fallen and consider ourselves as being vulnerable at the same time (Gal. 6:1).

We are prone to measure another person's faults and failures against the ones we would never be guilty of and judge their character against our own as long as our faults and failures are not discovered by the world. Jesus gave us a few severe warnings concerning this very issue. A person caught in the act of adultery is immediately judged by those who have not committed the physical act of adultery as having poor character. At the same time a person secretly lusting after someone who is not his or her spouse may never be found out. We may judge him or her as being a person of great character, yet Jesus judges them both as guilty of the same sin.

Likewise, we are quick to judge one who is guilty of killing another as a murderer and therefore flawed in his or her character. However, the apostle John tells us the one who is guilty of hating his brother is equally guilty of the same character flaw and the same sin.

> Ye have heard that it was said by them of old time, Thou shalt not commit adultery: But I say unto you, That whosoever looketh on a woman to lust after her hath committed adultery with her already in his heart. (Matt. 5:27–28)

> Whosoever hateth his brother is a murderer: and ye know that no murderer hath eternal life abiding in him. (1 John 3:15)

It has been said, "The church kills their own ..." and sadly enough, this statement rings true in the hearts of many fallen soldiers of the cross. When sin finds someone out and the church begins to reject him or her, the emotional, spiritual, and physical wounds caused not only by the sin but also by the rejection are deep.

Wounded soldiers of the cross are all around us, and the reasons are vast. Some are wounded because of their own sin. Some are wounded because others sin against them. Some are wounded from gossip or just down-right lies. Others are wounded because of poor communications, and still others are wounded from simple misunderstandings.

The reasons for a soldier being wounded may be unending, but the reason for the wound is not the point here. The point is, the wounded soldier—the one who has been bruised by life and feels hopeless to get back up—needs to be restored by those who are spiritual. We are instructed not to think too highly of ourselves and to bear one another's burdens (Gal. 6:2–3).

A simple review of our own lives and a quick glance in the mirror will reveal to all of us the truth about how easy it is to fall or fail and how bad it is for us when another person fires a shot of judgment in our direction. Life bruises all of us. The ability to get back up and keep going or the ability to keep trying in the face of rejection and judgment from others would be a better measurement of one's character than the measurement of failure. When we reach out in love to the wounded and fallen to bring them back, we help "save that soul from death" (James 5:19–20). It may surprise the church how many fallen soldiers would be willing to stand up again if the church would reach out to them in true love without condemnation or judgment.

Christ as the servant of God is the foundation on which all the promises of God are sanctioned, proven absolute, and made sure. The fullness of the Spirit of God was put upon Him, and all of Father God's power has been committed to Him, including the power of all judgment unto truth and victory. The church must take note the judgments that come from Jesus always result in victory, not defeat.

Both Isaiah and Matthew declared the faithful Servant of God will bring judgment yet will not break into pieces that which is bruised, and He will not quench even the tiniest ember of fire. The hurting, wounded, and bruised children of God are included in this promise. Even in our wounded beings the spark of God's Spirit remains resident within our spirits. We cannot hide, deny, or otherwise escape from the covenant God adopted us into because this covenant is His own Son, Jesus the Christ.

> I the LORD have called thee in righteousness, and will hold thine hand, and will keep thee, and give thee for a covenant of the people, for a light of the Gentiles. (Isa. 42:6)

We have been redeemed by His blood and forgiven of our sins according to the riches of His grace and not by our own righteousness (Eph. 1:7). The riches of His grace bring us all to victory, and it is only by such grace anyone from the human race is justified (just-as-if-I'd never sinned) by our Lord.

Accordingly, we find ourselves blessed with all spiritual blessings in heavenly places (things) in Him because He chose us before the foundation of the world. It was and still is the Father's good pleasure and His will to look at us through the finished work of His Faithful Servant, Jesus the Christ. When God looks at us through the finished work of Christ, He sees us as holy, without blame, and lavishes us with His great love. God accepts in the Beloved, and there is no other way for us to be reconciled to Him. We never earned our position because of our own holiness or through our own righteous acts. Upon our repentance, He adopted us into His family just as we were and started the cleaning-up process of our lives (Eph. 1:3–6).

The bruises of life will carry us into a greater understanding of the grace of God upon our reconciliation to the King of Kings. He is not finished with us when we fail Him. He still loves us, and we still have a purpose in His kingdom. We are accountable to bring all of our pain, all of our sin, all of our disappointments, and all of our excuses to the altar of repentance and there be restored to continue our work for the King.

At this great altar we will discover His mighty hand covering our bruises to heal them and not break them. We will discover His breath fanning the flame that remains in our spirits to bring them back to a roaring fire and never desiring to put us out. We will discover even though we have failed Him, He never failed us. Even though we have forsaken Him, He has never forsaken us. Even though we attempted to leave Him, He has never left us. At this great altar, we will discover His love is greater than we ever dreamed as He waits for us to get back up and show the lost and dying world our true character, the character of a warrior. It is the character of one who can sustain an otherwise-fatal wound and get back up because the fight isn't over till He calls us home.

Chapter 2

One Anothers

A Mouse Story

A mouse looked through the crack in the wall to see the farmer and his wife open a package. *What food might this contain?* the mouse wondered. He was devastated to discover it was a mousetrap. Retreating to the farmyard, the mouse proclaimed this warning: "There is a mousetrap in the house! There is a mousetrap in the house!"

The chicken clucked and scratched, raised her head, and said, "Mr. Mouse, I can tell this is a grave concern to you, but it is of no consequence to me. I cannot be bothered by it."

The mouse turned to the pig and told him, "There is a mousetrap in the house! There is a mousetrap in the house!"

The pig sympathized, but said, "I am so very sorry, Mr. Mouse, but there is nothing I can do about it but pray ... Be assured you are in my prayers."

The mouse turned to the cow and said, "There is a mousetrap in the house! There is a mousetrap in the house!"

The cow said, "Wow, Mr. Mouse. I'm sorry for you, but it's no skin off my nose."

So the mouse returned to the house, head down and dejected, to face the farmer's mousetrap … alone …

That very night a sound was heard throughout the house—the sound of a mousetrap catching its prey. The farmer's wife rushed to see what was caught. In the darkness, she did not see it. It was a venomous snake whose tail was caught in the trap.

The snake bit the farmer's wife. The farmer rushed her to the hospital. When she returned home, she still had a fever. Everyone knows you treat a fever with fresh chicken soup, so the farmer took his hatchet to the farmyard for the soup's main ingredient, but his wife's sickness continued. Friends and neighbors came to sit with her around the clock. To feed them, the farmer butchered the pig. But alas, the farmer's wife did not get well; she died. So many people came for her funeral that the farmer had the cow slaughtered to provide enough meat for all of them for the funeral luncheon. And the mouse looked upon it all from his crack in the wall with great sadness.

The next time you hear someone is facing a problem and think it doesn't concern you, remember—when one of us is threatened, we are all at risk. We are all involved in this journey called life. We must keep an eye out for one another and make an extra effort to encourage one another.

(Author Unknown)

One Body

For as the body is one, and hath many members, and all the members of that .one body, being many, are one body: so also *is* Christ. For by one Spirit are we all baptized into one body, whether *we be* Jews or Gentiles, whether *we be* bond or free; and have been all made to drink into one Spirit. For the body is not one member, but many. If the foot shall say, Because I am not the hand, I am not of the body; is it therefore not of the body? And if the ear shall say, Because I am not the eye, I am not of the body; is it therefore not of the body? If the whole body *were* an eye, where *were* the hearing? If the whole *were* hearing, where *were* the smelling? But now hath God set the members every one of them in the body, as it hath pleased him. And if they were all one member, where *were* the body? But now *are* *they* many members, yet but one body. And the eye cannot say unto the hand, I have no need of thee: nor again the head to the feet, I have no need of you. Nay, much more those members of the body, which seem to be more feeble, are necessary: And those *members* of the body, which we think to be less honourable, upon these we bestow more abundant honour; and our uncomely *parts* have more abundant comeliness. For our comely *parts* have no need: but God hath tempered the body together, having given more abundant honour to that *part* which lacked: That there should be no schism in the body; but *that* the members should have the same care one for another. And whether one member suffer, all the members suffer with it; or one member be honored, all the members rejoice with it. (1 Cor. 12:12–26)

Just as our natural body is one, we are created to be one in the body of Christ. As such, when one part (or person) in the body of Christ is wounded or hurting or has fallen, the rest of the body of Christ should react with sympathy, empathy, and love. The greatest part of the body of Christ turns away from wounded, fallen soldiers of the cross during their most difficult days of life. However, God has reserved at least one of His faithful children who is willing to stand with the hurting man or woman, pick him or her up, and love him or her regardless of guilt or innocence. These faithful children are used of God to help restore the hurting soldier of the cross because of their love for God. When they become one with the wounded, the wounded will be able to find enough strength to get back up and keep going. Here is a partial list God gives us as instructions on how to be one with each other.

1. Serve one another (Gal. 5:13).
2. Bear ye one another's burdens (Gal. 6:2)
3. Forbear one another in love (Eph. 4:2).
4. We are members one of another (Eph. 4:25).
5. Be kind and tenderhearted to one another (Eph. 4:32).
6. Submit to one to another (Eph. 5:21).
7. Forgive one another (Col. 3:13).
8. Teach and admonish one another (Col. 3:16).
9. Love one another (1 Thess. 3:12, 4:9, 1 Pet. 1:22, 1 John 3:11, 23, 4:7, 11–12, 2 John 1:5).
10. Comfort one another (1 Thess. 4:18).
11. Edify one another (1 Thess. 5:11).
12. Be subject one to another (1 Pet. 5:5).
13. Exhort one another daily (Heb. 3:13).
14. Assemble with one another (Heb. 10:25).
15. Confess your faults and pray for one another (James 5:16).
16. Have compassion for one another (1 Pet. 3:8).

17. Be hospitable to one another (1 Pet. 4:9).
18. Greet one another with a kiss of charity (1 Pet. 5:14).

As soon as the church—the body of Christ—begins to implement these "one anothers" as a normal way of life instead of rejecting our fallen and killing our wounded, we will come into the original design of God. We will become one mind—His mind, the mind of Christ. When the children of God are one mind and living as the mind of Christ, keeping the unity of the Spirit in the bond of peace, we will deprive Satan of his advantage over us. The Enemy desires to divide us, and he is willing to conquer us one at a time, but when we are one body and one mind, the Enemy is powerless against us (1 Pet. 3:13). When men of God became one with me, I was strengthened and ultimately able to begin my life of ministry once again. I am thankful God never casts His children aside.

One Mind

To become one mind means we will be in harmony, understand each other's feelings, have compassion on one another, and be knit together as one. The very core of our beings, our "guts," will become tenderhearted, sympathetic and begin to live with tender mercies toward each other. We will become men and women of unselfish character no longer seeking "our own" but instead desiring to help someone else. We will be busy fulfilling our callings and inheriting our blessings.

> Finally, *be ye* all of one mind, having compassion one of another, love as brethren, *be* pitiful, *be* courteous: not rendering evil for evil, or railing for railing (insults): but contrariwise blessing; knowing that ye are thereunto called, that ye should inherit a blessing. (1 Pet. 3:8–9)

Jesus prayed for us to be one just as He and the Father are one. As one, Jesus only said what the Father told Him to say and only did what the Father told Him to do (ref. John 5:19). Jesus was the bodily form of God the Father in every aspect of life. Jesus stated the purpose for us to be one in Him and the Father was so the world would believe He was sent by the Father. One of the great longings of the church today is to see the glory of God, yet the very glory we desire to see is hidden within our own lives. In His prayer, Jesus said we have been given the same glory the Father gave to Him so we could be one. When the church intentionally becomes one with each other, we will become perfect, and the manifestation of the glory of God will not only be seen within the church, but the world will also finally know God the Father sent Jesus the Son for our redemption.

> And now I am no more in the world, but these are in the world, and I come to thee.

Holy Father, keep through thine own name those whom thou hast given me, that they may be one, as we are. (John 17:11)

That they all may be one; as thou, Father, art in me, and I in thee, that they also may be one in us: that the world may believe that thou hast sent me. And the glory which thou gavest me I have given them; that they may be one, even as we are one: I in them, and thou in me, that they may be made perfect in one; and that the world may know that thou hast sent me, and hast loved them, as thou hast loved me. (John 17:21–23)

To be of one mind is to love as Christ loves and to receive as Christ receives and to forgive as Christ forgives (Rom. 15:5–7). We must purpose in our hearts to only do, say, and be good to others. We must rejoice with those who rejoice, weep with those who weep, and keep a humble opinion of ourselves as we reach down to pick up the fallen soldiers who need our help. We must avoid evil, do good, seek peace, and pursue it at the cost of our own emotions and "holiness." We must be in harmony with the entire body of Christ, strive for unity, have compassion, and bear each other's burdens. Our insides must yearn over the afflicted, and suffer when they suffer that we may intercede for their restoration, joy and happiness in the Lord. Notice this is not something

Don Shackelford

the Lord does. This is what we are commanded to do in honor of our King.

> Rejoice with them that do rejoice, and weep
> with them that weep. *Be* of the same mind
> one toward another. Mind not high things,
> but condescend to men of low estate. Be not
> wise in your own conceits. (Rom. 12:15–16)

Perfect Law of Liberty

The very nature of the gospel is to look like Jesus to someone else. We should never resent or resist an opportunity to plant seeds of grace, mercy, and forgiveness for the building of God's church and usher in the power of His kingdom in revival through humbling acts of showing His love to the hurting and wounded body of Christ. We must do God's Word not just hear God's Word because doing His word liberates us as well as the fallen ones. In fact, the writer James teaches us to continue doing God's word and not be someone who forgets God's Word brings us God's blessings. This is the law whereby we will be judged (ref. James 2:12).

> But be ye doers of the word, and not hearers
> only, deceiving your own selves. For if any
> be a hearer of the word, and not a doer, he
> is like unto a man beholding his natural face
> in a glass: For he beholdeth himself, and

18

goeth his way, and straightway forgetteth
what manner of man he was. But whoso
looketh into the perfect law of liberty, and
continueth *therein,* he being not a forgetful
hearer, but a doer of the work, this man shall
be blessed in his deed. (James 1:22–25)

A law refers to the will of God and a rule of life to be
followed by everyone. Such a law provides punishment
for transgressors while providing rewards for the obedient.
The perfect law of liberty—the law of love—calls us all to
a state of liberty and freedom. While sparing no one and
dealing with everyone, it is wholly free from all defects and
produces freedom from the servitude of sinful passions and
lusts. By "looking into" this law, the verse intimates we
will be paying close attention to it intently and earnestly,
giving it consideration of things beyond your eyes. What
we see is not always what God sees. We have to become
humble and stoop down from our opinions to search a
matter all the way to the bottom. We must search diligently
into the mind of God, not our own minds. When we are
ready to (or already have) help to condemn fallen soldiers
of the cross, God is still ready to restore them and complete
the work God alone started in them. Which side of this
judgment are we interested in being on?

For he that said, Do not commit adultery,
said also, Do not kill. Now if you commit
no adultery, yet if you kill, you are become a

transgressor of the law. So speak you, and so do, as they that shall be judged by the law of liberty. For he shall have judgment without mercy, that hath shewed no mercy; and mercy rejoiceth against judgment. (James 2:11–13)

The path of duty is the way of safety and happiness. Whoever obeys God from a loving heart and pure conscience will without fail find continual blessings by the very act of keeping the perfect law of liberty (love). It will produce peace in our conscience and impart the highest order of happiness to our minds (one mind). It is the only way to have the mind of Christ active in our minds and to show the world the manifested glory of God. The perfect law of love is always perfecting us while providing the fullness of salvation established by faith and giving us power over sin, dominion over the enemy, and the influence of heaven itself.

We should strongly encourage one another to lead a holy life knowing we will be judged by a law where we will be free from the bondage of sin.

Chapter 3

Don't Bury the
Wounded Too Soon

The LORD is gracious, and full of
compassion; slow to anger, and of great
mercy. (Ps. 145:8)

Chocolate Chip Cookies

An elderly man was very ill and lay in his bed, fully expecting
to die at any time. In death's agony, he suddenly smelled
the aroma of his favorite chocolate chip cookies wafting
up the stairs. The smell was so overwhelming that he
somehow managed to gather his remaining strength to
lift himself from the bed. Leaning against the wall, he
slowly made his way out of the bedroom, and with even
greater effort, he forced himself down the stairs, gripping
the railing with both hands.

With labored breath, agony, and pain from the excursion,
he leaned against the kitchen doorframe for rest and gazed

into the room. Were it not for his physical pain, he would have thought himself already in heaven because there, spread out upon newspapers on the kitchen table, were literally hundreds of his favorite chocolate chip cookies. Was it heaven? Or was it one final act of heroic love from his devoted wife, seeing to it that he left this world a happy man? Mustering one great final effort, he threw himself toward the table, landing on his knees in a rumpled posture. His parched lips parted as he began to imagine the taste of the wondrous cookies already in his mouth. The thought actually invigorated him, seemingly bringing him back to life. His old and aged hand slowly made its way to a cookie at the edge of the table when it was suddenly smacked with a spatula by his wife. "Stay out of those," she snapped. "They're for the funeral." (http://www.cleanjokeoftheday. com/jokes-funeralcookies.html)

(Author unknown)

Fallen but Not Forsaken

It is obvious the Lord wants us to walk together, work together, and live as a family together. We are designed just like He is. When one part of the body hurts, the whole body hurts. When we have infirmities, He feels our pain. When a Christian falls, the entire body comes under the scrutiny of the world, and we are all mocked. Our natural tendency is to isolate the "wound" and try to continue life as well as we possibly can. To our embarrassment, we immediately cast aside the fallen. We shake our heads in disbelief, assemble ourselves together against them, and brace for the world's charges against the rest of us. We distance ourselves from the guilty people, and in disgust, we judge them as unbelievable failures. Such actions are equivalent to cutting off a finger or a toe that has sustained the injury of a splinter instead of removing the splinter and mending the wound. What would the reaction of the world be if the body of Christ ran to surround, protect, and restore fallen comrades instead of rejecting them?

God has joined us to His family, and He is not so quick to cast us aside. Instead of forsaking us, He pursues us. He is slow to anger, renews His plentiful mercy every day, continues to pour His grace over us, and has compassion for us in the midst of our failures.

> Whither shall I go from thy spirit? or whither shall I flee from thy presence? If I ascend up into heaven, thou art there: if I make my bed in hell, behold, thou art there. If I take the wings of the morning, and dwell in the uttermost parts of the sea; Even there shall thy hand lead me, and thy right hand shall hold me. If I say, Surely the darkness shall cover me; even the night shall be light about me. Yea, the darkness hideth

not from thee; but the night shineth as the
day: the darkness and the light are both alike
to thee. (Ps. 139:7–12)

When the Lord was dealing with Israel in the days of
Nehemiah, the people were full of pride, which the Lord
hates. They hardened their hearts and stiffened their necks,
and in their rebellion, they refused to obey Him. They
even appointed a captain to return them to bondage. Even
then, God was ready to pardon them, show them grace
and mercy, be slow to anger against them, and show them
great kindness, and He refused to forsake them. They are
His family, His chosen, His body (Neh. 9).

When souls are born again, they are born into the family
of God and are entered into His family covenant records.
They are adopted into the loins of Abraham and become
His body. As a part of the body of Christ, He knows every
one of us personally. He never forsakes any of us, even
when we forsake Him. God is Faithful unto the end, and
His faithfulness is never weighed against our ability to
deserve Him. In His faithfulness, the Lord is constantly
busy about rebuilding us after rebirthing us.

For ye have not received the spirit of bondage
again to fear; but ye have received the Spirit
of adoption, whereby we cry, Abba, Father.
(Rom. 8:15)

To redeem them that were under the law,
that we might receive the adoption of sons.
(Gal. 4:5)

Having predestinated us unto the adoption
of children by Jesus Christ to himself,
according to the good pleasure of his will.
(Eph. 1:5)

Like the white blood cells of our natural bodies that run to
the aid of a wound within our bodies, the church should
respond to fallen soldiers of the cross and run to the aid of
the wounded ones to repair and restore them.

The Righteous Religious Attitude

Here is the essence of what a righteous religious spirit
sounds like: "These fallen have fallen and are no longer
worthy to be counted as viable men or women of God.
They can never stand in the pulpits or government
offices of the unfallen because they have fallen, and by
their fall, they have proven their lack of character to the
unfallen. How dare they want to stand in the same pulpit
or government office as the unfallen and lead a world of
other sinners into the grace of God?

"If these fallen attempt to get back up, there will be plenty
of the unfallen to condemn them for even trying. If these
fallen are caught repenting, their repentance has to be

proven to the unfallen. At a minimum there must be some time between their repentance and them ever reaching for an office of leadership again. It is important for us unfallen to find these fallen to be restorable and then restored by the unfallen before these fallen can resume a position of authority within the community or the kingdom of God. After all ... they are fallen; how dare they try again?

"The fallen can never be leaders again. They just need to stay down for the count. There is no need to attempt to restore the fallen; the righteous religious will never trust them again anyway. Who do they think they are? Just stay down and let the unfallen church handle the fallen, sinful world. Do these dead dry bones actually believe they can live again?"

For the unfallen church to reject the fallen church is equal to the unfallen church forgetting where they came from themselves. Jesus didn't come to condemn the world. He came to save the world. At what point in our Christian journey did the Lord appoint the righteous religious unfallen church to be the condemners of the fallen church? The unfallen church is instructed to meekly and gently restore the fallen and while restoring them and take a good look at themselves lest they become the fallen.

Our Re-Creator

Jesus loves sinners. If He didn't, where would *you* be right now? Our human nature tells us we need to "be good enough" for God to use us. When the apostle Peter first realized Jesus was a man of God, his immediate assumption was the Lord wouldn't want anything to do with him. Peter said, "I'm too much of a sinner to be around you. "Please leave" (Luke 5:1–10).

In our human nature, we want to make ourselves presentable and earn God's forgiveness before we come to Him and we have an uncanny way of trying to place that same requirement on others. The Lord, however, tells us to come just as we are. Fixing our lives first wasn't possible when we came to the Lord for salvation, so why do we demand the fallen church to be good enough before they are fully restored to our fellowship? God the Father is the only being who can decide when we are good enough for His work, and He decided we reached that point when we were still sinners.

> But God commendeth his love toward us, in that, while we were yet sinners, Christ died for us. (Rom. 5:8)

Jesus passed right by the religious groups and went into the houses and lives of sinners. He ate with tax collectors, drank water with adulterers, and allowed fallen women to wash His feet with their hair. He touched the demon possessed, the lepers, the blind, the crippled, and as many less thans as He could find. He recreated every one of their lives, and when they failed Him and forsook Him,

He never said they had to do enough, spend enough time doing enough, or fix all their failures before He would forgive them, heal them, or restore them. Upon an encounter with Him, they were fully restored in a right relationship to Him. No amount of time had to pass, and they were never required to prove anything to Him or anyone else. They were already recreated, and now they were being restored to the wholeness He rebirthed them at the time of their salvation.

God is our re-Creator, our Justifier, and our Elector, so who would dare condemn one of the family of God because he or she has fallen into sin, even within the church? Yet every one of us is guilty of casting off the fallen and harshly judging them because their sin (revealed) is different than our sin (hidden). When the Lord weighs our sins, even the hidden sin, against the price of the blood of His Son, we are found innocent upon repentance! He is busy changing sinners into saints, and it's not by our own doings or our own lives or our own righteousness. It is by His own re-creating works through the resurrection power of the blood of His Son, Jesus the Christ.

The entire religious community might write off the fallen individual, but God who is faithful will use your mess and make it His message to a lost and dying world. He is calling you to make a difference in this world, and He will use your failures to carry you to a more noble purpose if you will let Him. Peter was changed from a man who denied knowing the Lord because he was afraid for his life into a man who would stand on the street corners and preach this same Jesus because his life was at stake.

Peter entered into a greater ministry after he failed the Lord than he ever had before he failed the Lord. Likewise, He will use the one returning to Him from a fallen state even greater than before. He will use your body to perform His works, your hands to help the helpless, your eyes to focus on His glory, your tongue to speak His blessings, your lips to spread His gospel, your feet to carry His truth to the nations, your heart to mend the broken, your tears to heal the hurting, and your life to build His family for the sake of His kingdom on the earth.

Francis Frangipane said, "No confessing sinner was ever isolated from the Messiah's grace; no sin or flaw rendered one exiled from the mercy's reach. Only one type of person consistently found himself outside Christ's transforming power: the hypocrite. A hypocrite is a master of disguises." (Quoted from Francis Frangipane on Facebook)

The Story of Betsy, the Mule.

There was a farmer who had a mule named Betsy. Betsy worked hard for the farmer all the days of her life. Then one day the farmer went down to Tunica, Mississippi— and won big on the nickel slot machines. He went out and bought himself one of those big John Deere tractors, and he didn't need old Betsy to till his garden. So Betsy sat idle and grew old—and the farmer decided he didn't want her around anymore. But he wasn't man enough to shoot old Betsy in the head as they do cattle in their old age. So he decided to dig a ditch. He climbed up in his new tractor and pushed old Betsy in. He started to shovel, filling the hole with dirt. He wasn't man enough to watch as he tried to bury poor Betsy alive, so he turned his back and proceeded to shovel, filling the hole with dirt.

But old Betsy, down in that hole, look up as the dirt came down on her head, and she just shook it off and stomped it under her feet. Meanwhile, the farmer kept pitching the dirt—but old Betsy kept looking up and shaking it off and stomping it down. When the farmer finished with the dirt, he turned around, and there was old Betsy staring him in the face (author unknown).

If you are the fallen and the church or the world has rendered you no longer valuable to work for the King, then repent, rest, and be restored. God is not ready to bury you, so don't allow anyone else to bury you either. Get up and get busy for your King. If you are the one guilty of rendering a fallen soldier of the cross no longer useful to the King and have condemned him or her to being a failure and a person of poor character, then you should quickly consider yourself, ask the Lord to search your heart, and see if there are any wicked ways in you. Then repent and reach out to restore your comrade to the

King's service before you become the fallen soldier and find yourself in need of a loving heart and a helping hand.

Search me, O God, and know my heart: try me, and know my thoughts: And see if there be any wicked way in me, and lead me in the way everlasting. (Ps. 139:23–24)

Chapter 4

Looking Like Christians

And when he had found him, he brought him unto Antioch. And it came to pass, that a whole year they assembled themselves with the church, and taught much people. And the disciples were called Christians first in Antioch. (Acts 11:26)

The Goose

A nineteenth-century Danish philosopher, Søren Kierkegaard, told a story about a goose who was wounded and who landed in a barnyard with some chickens. The goose played with the chickens and ate with the chickens and slept with the chickens. After a while that goose thought he was a chicken. One day a flight of geese flew over, migrating to their home. As geese do, they honked and honked and honked. The goose in the barnyard heard it and "something stirred [deep] within the breast of this goose. That something called him to the skies. He began to flap the wings he hadn't used, and he rose a few feet into the air. Then he stopped, and he settled back again into the mud of the barnyard. He heard the cry, but he settled for less." (http://www.sermoncentral.com/ illustrations/sermon-illustration-mark-roper-stories-call-vision-motivation-1649.asp)

Research says when a goose is wounded during flight and cannot keep up with the flock, two other geese will stay with the wounded or ill bird until he dies or is strong enough to rejoin the flock. When Christians go down for the count, those who are around them are called by God to restore them, carry their burdens, and otherwise consider themselves lest they become the fallen. We are called to put our own pleasures aside and help bear the infirmities (misgivings, regrets) of the weak.

When souls come to the Lord for salvation, they bring everything they have to offer the Lord in exchange for the free gift. We find ourselves able to offer Him the bodies we have worn out, abused, and filled with poisons, the minds we have used to constantly think of evil deeds, our hands we have used to commit evil acts, and our eyes we have used to lust after idolatrous and adulterous objects. In addition to these wonderful gifts, we offer Him our tongues we have used for lying and cursing as well as our feet we have used to run from Him and into the mischief of the world. Graciously, He accepts our offer, scrubs us clean by the shed blood of His Son, and then gives us His mercy and justification in exchange.

Because of this incredible cleansing and exchanging of His life for ours, it should be an honor for us to stand by the side of a fallen comrade, remembering where we came from ourselves. Even though we have been washed by the blood of Jesus Christ, we remember the days our hearts were filled with hatred, anger, grief, and sin. We remember our old selfish ways, self-centered desires, and self-gratifying lifestyles.

The Enemy is always seeking someone to devour and destroy. As our hearts remember where we came from, we dare not cast aside another who has fallen prey to the enemy of our souls but reach out and to restore them just like Jesus reached down for us and is reaching now for them.

The responsibility for our lives always lies personally upon each of us, and we will all give an account unto the Lord "on that day." Therefore the fallen have the responsibility to properly respond when restoration, help, forgiveness, and love are offered by the church.

When restoration is offered, we must encourage the faith seed that is deep within the spirit of wounded soldiers that God still loves them, cares for them, and has a destiny and a destination for them. We must help the wounded to look toward God's glory in the heavens, hold onto His mercy that is renewed every day, trust in the grace that is still freely given to them, and remind them God is willing and able to finish what He started in them.

The Lord has a plan and a path for each one of us. When one strays from one's path, it does not change God's plan. We must stay together, work together, and finish together because we are on this journey together, and we are *one* in Him.

Condemnation and rejection are the Enemy's tools and should never be used by the church of Jesus Christ. They are heavy tools that cause much destruction and are designed to destroy a soul. The impact upon a human soul can be greater than death himself. It leaves one feeling as though death would be easier, and many people wish, even pray, to die when they are afflicted with condemnation and rejection. Jesus did not come to condemn anyone. As Christians (Christlike-ians), we should never condemn or reject the fallen. We must strive to heal them, restore them, and reunite with them.

Christlike-Ians

God breathed into clay formed by His own hands, giving His life to Adam, and said it was *very good!* Then Adam decided he wanted knowledge over life and sold God out for a piece of fruit. That made God *very sad.* A few thousand years later, God breathed into the womb of a virgin piece of clay named Mary and gave His life to a second Adam named Jesus. That made God *very happy.* Thirty-three years later, Satan snuffed out the life of the second Adam. That made God *very sad.* Three days later, God breathed life back into the second Adam when he resurrected Jesus from the dead. That made God *very happy* ... In fact, it made Him *so happy* that God said, "I want a whole bunch more just like you!" So He created Christlike people in Antioch and then continued to multiply His new creation all over the world!

Christians Defined

Followers of Christ, anointed by God, consecrated to an office, furnished with what is needed to act toward another in the same manner as Christ would act ... Christlike, once dead in sin, now alive in Christ. Crucified with Him, now alive by Him. One whose old life is buried with Him in baptism and whose new life is risen in Him to be like Him. One who has all things made new, knows the love of God that is beyond knowing, and is filled with the fullness of God.

> I am crucified with Christ: nevertheless I live; yet not I, but Christ liveth in me: and the life which I now live in the flesh I live by the faith of the son of god, who loved me, and gave himself for me. (Gal. 2:20)

> Therefore we are buried with him by baptism into death: that like as Christ was raised up from the dead by the glory of the Father,

even so we also should walk in newness of life. (Rom. 6:4)

Buried with him in baptism, wherein also ye are risen with him through the faith of the operation of God, who hath raised him from the dead. (Col. 2:12)

Therefore if any man be in Christ, he is a new creature: old things are passed away; behold, all things are become new. (2 Cor. 5:17).

And to know the love of Christ, which passeth knowledge, that ye might be filled with all the fulness of God. (Eph. 3:19)

The name *Christian* unites nations, removes socioeconomic barriers, and binds all of humanity together. In short, it bonds us into one family. In the family we must walk worthy of the family name and never disgrace our Father. In the family, everyone is subject to the Father, and no one is supreme over another family member. To walk worthy of the name Christian brings us to the challenge of how we should deal with those who have disgraced our family name. The answer will always go back to the Father's wishes, designs, and ways. The Father always loves us. The Father always forgives us. The Father always restores us, and the Father is always doing good for us, to us, and with us.

> That ye would walk worthy of God, who hath called you unto his kingdom and glory. (1 Thess. 2:12)

Chapter 5

Life in the Wounds

And not only *so,* but we glory in tribulations also: knowing that tribulation worketh patience; And patience, experience; and experience, hope: And hope maketh not ashamed; because the love of God is shed abroad in our hearts by the Holy Ghost which is given unto us. (Rom. 5:3–5)

A Butterfly

One day a small opening appeared on a cocoon. A man sat and watched the butterfly for several hours as it struggled to force its body through that little opening. Then it seemed to stop making any progress. It appeared as if it had gotten as far as it could and it could go no further. So the man decided to help the butterfly. He took a pair of scissors and snipped off the remaining bit of the cocoon. The butterfly then emerged easily. But it had a swollen body and small, shriveled wings. The man continued to watch the butterfly because he expected that, at any moment, the wings would expand to be able to support the body, which would contract in time.

Neither happened. In fact, the butterfly spent the rest of its life crawling around with a swollen body and shriveled wings. It never was able to fly. What the man in his kindness and haste did not understand was that the restricting cocoon and the struggle required for the butterfly to get through the opening were God's way of forcing the fluid from the body of the butterfly into its wings so it would be ready for flight once it achieved its freedom from the cocoon.

Sometimes struggles are exactly what we need in life. If God allowed us to go through life without any obstacles, it would cripple us. We would not be as strong as we could have been. We could never fly.

When others wound us, the Lord blesses us, and great rewards wait for us in heaven. The wounds of life can actually bring us life as the Lord faithfully prunes away the deadness of our flesh. As the butterfly is forced to push his way through the cocoon to give his wings the strength to fly, our struggles force us to push through trying times while we discover what God means when He says His strength is made perfect in our weakness. In our infirmities the power of Christ will rest upon us. It is through tribulations we learn of our inability and God's great ability.

I am the true vine, and my Father is the husbandman. Every branch in me that beareth not fruit he taketh away: and every branch that beareth fruit, he purgeth it, that it may bring forth more fruit. (John 15:1–2)

Blessed are ye, when men shall revile you, and persecute you, and shall say all manner of evil against you falsely, for my sake. Rejoice, and be exceeding glad: for great is your reward in heaven: for so persecuted they the prophets which were before you. (Matt. 5:11–12)

And he said unto me, My grace is sufficient for thee: for my strength is made perfect in weakness. Most gladly therefore will I rather glory in my infirmities, that the power of Christ may rest upon me. (2 Cor. 12:9)

We should not pray for easier paths to walk but for faith to walk the path the Lord has us in. Even when we are in the path of the valley of the shadow of death, the Lord is still the one leading us. When we follow Him, we will be safe. The Lord who is directing us is infinitely wise and knows what we need to be victorious over life and all of the circumstances we face—even when we bring problems and troubles on ourselves.

Jesus is our Lord. We can trust Him, have faith in Him, put our hope in Him, and have an expectation of Him to keep us safe and deliver us whole to the Father.

A Wounded Church

As I was writing this chapter, my phone rang. On the other end was the voice of a very excited young lady who just happens to be my daughter, Crystal. She was excited because the call God put in her heart was about to be fulfilled. One year ago we were discussing her dilemma. God called her to be a youth leader. Her local church is a small community church that loves the Lord with all their heart but is trapped with a few religious ideas that seemed to prevent some members from fulfilling their calls from God. The by-laws of this church prevented a divorced person from having a place of leadership within the congregation, so she never voiced her heart to the leaders. In other words, the by-laws appeared to say, "If you have fallen in the past, you have no business leading others in the church." Since both the husband and wife were divorced in the past, there was no need to pursue a position as the youth leaders. Her heart was disappointed, but she refused to allow her spirit to be dampened. Along with her husband, she decided to just serve the present leadership in whatever capacity they would be allowed and faithfully did so for the remaining time.

Then it happened. A week ago, approximately one year after discussing the dilemma with us, and a few hours before their summer VBS was about to start, without notice, the pastor of the church, the youth leaders, and some of the other families announced they were leaving the congregation to follow the Lord in some other capacity. The wounds within the congregation were deep and extremely painful. Most of the remaining members were confused as well as wounded and were left bleeding on the battlefield without their leaders.

My daughter and son-in-law and a few others rose to the occasion and followed through with VBS instead of canceling the event. At the end of their VBS, another situation was brought to their attention. The youth had been working diligently to afford a trip to the local theme park, and they had raised the necessary funds to go but now the youth leaders had left the church. Wounded, discouraged, confused, and bleeding on the spiritual battlefield, Crystal and her husband decided to rise to the occasion and take these kids to their planned event.

Now, through their wounds (the people who decided to leave the church without a forewarning), Crystal became alive with excitement while preparing to fulfill the call of God in her life. Sometimes even a church has to be pruned of its religious branches so the branches that were having the life choked out of them can grow. Below is a story Crystal just sent me about the Lord speaking to her.

Crystal's Rose Bush Story

I only write this story because my husband asked me to. This is a recent conversation I had with my heavenly Father on a Friday when I needed to hear from Him.

It had been a very long week! We attend a small church nearby that is home to family and friends and loved ones galore. Doyle and I had been attending church there as early as our toddler years. As life would have it, we both wandered far from God but found Him again and returned at different times, finding one another in the process. We have many memories and life changes there, and spiritually we thrived there, feeling God's presence over and over again for more than four years.

On this particular Sunday, our pastor had stepped down and left our church in an unexpected way. He took with him some strong leaders and families of the church. We were sad, brokenhearted, and confused. We cried right along with our children and tried to explain to them what was going on. Through all the tears and broken hearts, we still felt God with us, leading us and telling us to continue His work there more than ever before.

You might think I sound crazy! My earthly father does this all the time; he tells a story about talking to God like he's having a conversation, just like He was a man standing next to him. I have always thought, *Huh, we don't talk like that; God and I.* But this day would be different!

As it goes, I was weeding our small flower bed out in front of our home. I began to pray. "Lord please strengthen our little church ... keep hearts pure. Show our children that faith will move mountains. Help me to hear You. I pray for guidance during this rough transition. You know my heart." Along those lines, I just began to talk to him and speak my true heart.

Then out of the blue, God just spoke to me and said, "Go tend to that rose bush!" I glanced over and thought, *Wow that bush was just full of flowers.* It had been beautiful, with ten or so blooms and flowers in full pink glory. Now it looked like a dying bush being choked out by the dead pieces left from those same blooms. God said again, "Tend to that rose bush!" I went to it. Upon further inspection, I could see new growth trying to make its way upward and dead, decayed branches just getting in the way. God said, "Remove the dead branches." I said, "But God, there is some new growth nearby, and I don't want to remove budding parts of the bush." He said, "Do as I say. It will be better for the bush as a whole in the long run. It might look rough for a little while, but you must clean it out completely!" I clipped off more than I wanted to, but I was trying to listen as best as I could.

God then led me to the bottom, where dead and healthy parts of the bush met. There sat a large piece of root that looked to me as if it was important to the growth of the bush as a whole. God then said, "Cut that off!"

"But I can't! It needs to be there!"

"No, child, just apply a small amount of pressure."

I was obedient and did as I was told. That "important" piece was rotten and dried out and came off with the slightest bit of pressure, not affecting the bush as a whole at all. Then He said, "Now clean off that bark at the bottom. Expose as much of the true bush as you can, and don't forget to be gentle." I took the clippers in hand and began to scrape away the decay and rot. As I did, a hundred or more pill bugs (or roly-polys, as we call them) began to scatter like nothing I have ever seen before! I don't know if you know much about that type of bug, but they love dark areas where they can hide away and eat decaying plants. They were killing my rose bush, and I didn't even know until God directed me to take notice.

When I finally sat back and looked at what was left, my eyes began to tear up. God's guidance made a perfectly healthy yet slim rose bush ready for new growth and blooms. There was one very strong branch with a few smaller ones jutting off of it. It was so strong that the wind was blowing and it did not move. Also left were five or so additional branches bending a bit in the wind but strong and ready to bloom if given the chance.

As I cleaned up the pieces that were left on the ground, I was pricked with a thorn. God said to me, "See, My child, sometimes the cleanup hurts, but it must be done. I am in control!"

It does not take one man or one family but an entire family of God to strengthen His house. Sometimes the parts that looked so important were not ready for a little pressure and needed to be taken out of that place for the rest of the willing pieces to perform properly. We will continue to look to God above for guidance and strength during this time of change. But just like this rose bush, we will bloom and grow and be strong for our Lord Jesus.
~crystal huth, 06/17/2013~

Chapter 6

God Is For Us

God Uses Problems

What shall we then say to these things? If God
be for us, who *can be* against us? (Rom. 8:31)

We must change our way of thinking. We have to focus
not only on who God is but also what His heart is toward
us as His children. God is on our side. The manner in
which we see God will determine the manner in which
we will see ourselves and the manner in which we deal
with others, especially the fallen soldiers of the cross. God
is not mad at us. He is attempting to pour His mercy upon
us because He understands our temple of clay is naturally
wicked by Adam's nature in us (Rom. 5:8).

If we see God as a religious, judging, angry, and controlling
person, we will become a religious, judging, angry, and
controlling church. I fear many of us have entered into
seeing God in this manner, though we are not even aware of
it ourselves. If we see God as a merciful, loving, forgiving,

and restoring person, we will become a merciful, loving, forgiving, and restoring church. Most of the local churches teach God is the latter when they are trying to reach a lost world, and when a member of the body of Christ falls or fails, they act as though God is the former. The truth is, on the one hand God is a demanding God; it will be His way or no way. On the other hand, He is our Gentle Shepherd, leading a frightened and cantankerous people to His eternal bliss.

The Lord is holy, just, and righteous, and He will judge us on that day. Meanwhile He uses our faults, our failures, and our problems to equip us, build endurance in our lives, and teach us who He is as He draws us closer to Himself.

God is our El Shaddai, meaning He is the all-sufficient, more than enough, breasted one. It is a name He attributes to Himself to help us recognize He has a love for us like our own mother's love. His love pulls us to His bosom to provide us strength, nourishment, and emotional support just like a mother would provide for her newborn baby at her own breasts. He is strong enough to supply our every need, sensitive enough to care for us when we hurt, and tender enough to love us even when we fail Him. Interestingly enough, Scripture uses the name El Shaddai (almighty God) exclusively when discussing God in relationship with His children.

He that dwelleth in the secret place of the most High shall abide under the shadow of the (El Shaddai) Almighty. (Ps. 91:1)

As our almighty God He is our Provider, Deliverer, Healer, Comforter, Peace Maker, Peace Giver, High Tower, Rock, Anchor, Savior, and Lover of our Souls. He is also light in our darkness and a Light to light our way.

He is our Redeemer, our Savior, our Guide, and He is our Peace! In addition to all of that, He is our Joy, Comfort, and Lord. He will never leave us, never forsake us, never mislead us, and never forget us. When we fall, He lifts us up; when we fail, He forgives us; and when we are weak, He is strong! When we are lost, He is the way; when we are afraid, He is our courage; when we stumble, He steadies us; when we are hurt, He heals us; and when we are broken, He mends us! When we are blind, He leads us; when we are hungry, He feeds us; when we face trials, He is with us; when we face persecution, He shields us; when we face problems, He comforts us; when we face loss, He provides for us; and when we face death, He carries us home! He is God, and He is Faithful. We are His, and He is ours!

If we had no problems, we would not come to know God, and if we never had questions, we would never need answers. Trouble will stop when it accomplishes the purpose God allowed it to come for in the first place.

Run to the Mercy Seat

It is an interesting thing to consider what God told Moses to do with the second set of the Ten Commandments. Moses broke the first tablets when he saw the wickedness and sin of Israel. But God told Moses to place the second set of tablets in the ark of the covenant (Deut. 10:2, 5). Inside the ark of the covenant the law of God would be hidden from the eyes of everyone, including God Himself. In fact when God would look down from heaven upon the ark, He would be looking at the mercy seat with the sacrificial blood sprinkled on it and not the law contained inside of the ark.

The story of the woman caught in the very act of adultery recorded in John 8:1–11 teaches us about God's desires to show us mercy and not judgment.

> Jesus went unto the mount of Olives. And early in the morning he came again into the temple, and all the people came unto him; and he sat down, and taught them. And the scribes and Pharisees brought unto him a woman taken in adultery; and when they had set her in the midst, they say unto him, Master, this woman was taken in adultery, in the very act. This they said, tempting him, that they might have to accuse him. But Jesus stooped down, and

with his finger wrote on the ground, as though he heard them not. So when they continued asking him, he lifted up himself, and said unto them, He that is without sin among you, let him first cast a stone at her. And again he stooped down, and wrote on the ground. And they which heard it, being convicted by their own conscience, went out one by one, beginning at the eldest, even unto the last: and Jesus was left alone, and the woman standing in the midst. When Jesus had lifted up himself, and saw none but the woman, he said unto her, Woman, where are those thine accusers? hath no man condemned thee? She said, No man, Lord. And Jesus said unto her, Neither do I condemn thee: go, and sin no more. (John 8:1–11)

Jesus had every legal right to condemn this woman by the law but chose mercy over judgment. Whatever He wrote in the sand, along with His challenge for the sinless to cast the first stone, caused every man there to be convicted by their own consciences, drop their stones, walk away, and also choose mercy over judgment.

The church would be wise to take this story to heart and follow this example when they are faced with needing to deal with a fallen soldier of the cross. We should not only run to the mercy seat ourselves but also help the fallen run there as well. God's mercy is waiting for all of us. The Lord looks upon the shed blood of His Son Jesus before He looks upon the law.

Chapter 7

Running the Race

What Is Really Important?

Know ye not that they which run in a race
run all, but one receiveth the prize? So run,
that ye may obtain. (1 Cor. 9:24)

Teach Us to Run the Race

I remember a story about the hundred-yard dash at the
Seattle Special Olympics. Nine contestants, all physically
or mentally disabled, assembled at the starting line for
the hundred-yard dash. When the gun sounded, they
all started out with a relish to run the race to the finish
and win.

One little boy stumbled on the asphalt, tumbled over a
couple of times, and began to cry. The other eight heard
the boy cry. They slowed down and looked back! Then
they all turned around and went back, every one of them.
One girl with Down's syndrome bent down and kissed him

and said, "This will make it better." Then all nine linked arms and walked to the finish line together. Everyone in the stadium stood, and the cheering went on for several minutes. People who were there are still telling the story.

Is running the race of life important enough to leave someone behind to win, or is it more important to bring as many runners to the finish line with you as you possibly can? This road of life is full of trip hazards, failures, and tragedies that will ultimately wound us. Sometimes our fellow comrades stumble and will need help getting back up. We would be wise to remember every action of our lives can be equated to sowing seeds, and whatever seeds we sow we will reap. If we sow seeds of compassion, love, tenderness, caring, and restoring, we will receive a harvest of compassion, love, tenderness, caring, and restoring when we need it. If we sow seeds of judgment, hatred, strife, and grief, we will receive a harvest of judgment, hatred, strife, and grief in a time when we don't need it. Our goal is eternity, and our desire should be to bring as many souls with us as possible.

Righteous men fall, but it does not exclude them from the service of the King. The Lord Himself will hold him up and sustain him. Who dares to turn his or her back on someone the Lord is holding in His own hand?

> For a just man falleth seven times, and riseth up again ... (Prov. 24:16)

The steps of a good man are ordered by
the LORD: and he delighteth in his way.
Though he fall, he shall not be utterly cast
down: for the LORD upholdeth him with
his hand. (Ps. 37:23–24)

The Story Of Jonah

The story of Jonah shows the grace of God to a Gentile
nation and a jealous Jew who wanted them to suffer for
their sin at the hand of God's judgment. God wanted
Ninevah to have mercy through repentance. Jonah wanted
them to die in their sins. God showed mercy to both sinner
and grumbling saint.

The word pictures in this story are great examples for the
church to consider when dealing with a fallen soldier of
the cross. God wants them to repent, and too often the
church wants them to suffer because of their failures and
sins, especially if the failure was against another member
of the kingdom.

The name *Jonah* signifies a "dove," and Jesus instructs us
to be harmless as doves (Matt. 10:16). It is noteworthy to
mention the sins of Nineveh "came up before the Lord"
and were never denied or overlooked. They were first
proclaimed by the man of God and then offered to be
removed through repentance. At no time in this writing
have I suggested we should overlook the sin of the fallen as

though it never happened. What is important to remember is the heart of God to restore the fallen soldier of the cross and enter into His restorative process, never judging, never condemning, always remaining humble, and always loving like you want to be loved.

All Punishment from God Is Restorative In Nature

Now the word of the LORD came unto Jonah the son of Amittai, saying, Arise, go to Nineveh, that great city, and cry against it; for their wickedness is come up before me. But Jonah rose up to flee unto Tarshish from the presence of the LORD, and went down to Joppa; and he found a ship going to Tarshish: so he paid the fare thereof, and went down into it, to go with them unto Tarshish from the presence of the LORD. But the LORD sent out a great wind into the sea, and there was a mighty tempest in the sea, so that the ship was like to be broken. (Jonah 1:1–4)

Now the LORD had prepared a great fish to swallow up Jonah. And Jonah was in the belly of the fish three days and three nights. (Jonah 1:17)

> And said, I cried by reason of mine affliction
> unto the LORD, and he heard me; out of
> the belly of hell cried I, and thou heardest
> my voice. (Jonah 2:2)

> But I will sacrifice unto thee with the voice
> of thanksgiving; I will pay that that I have
> vowed. Salvation is of the LORD. (Jonah 2:9)

When we begin to think what we do does not matter or that we can "get away with it," God pursues us, often trouble overtakes us, our sins are revealed, and we become miserable because nothing goes right for us. God gives us spankings as a loving Father, but they are never to harm us. They are only meant to bring us back to the knowledge of how miserable we are without Him and to redirect our steps back to His service. Trouble is meant to bring us greater faith as it pushes us toward an altar of repentance and forces us to reach our limited hands up to grab hold of His limitless hand and trust Him as our heavenly Father.

> The LORD hath his way in the whirlwind
> and in the storm, and the clouds are the dust
> of his feet. (Nahum 1:3b)

The church is instructed to fulfill the law of Christ by bearing one another's burdens. He bore our sins, not His, and carried them on His shoulders to the cross. In return we are required to bear burdens that are not our own to help our fellow man win the victory of life. We must treat others as we want to be treated. When we are hurting deep inside, we want someone to care, someone to cry with us, and someone to help us. In the case of fallen brothers, they need burden-bearing friends, not condemning, judging, religious people around them. This is what is important. This is how to run and win the race set before us.

> Bear ye one another's burdens, and so fulfil the law of Christ. (Gal. 6:2)

> Therefore all things whatsoever ye would that men should do to you, do ye even so to them: for this is the law and the prophets. (Matt. 7:12)

> Hereby perceive we the love of God, because he laid down his life for us: and we ought to lay down our lives for the brethren. But whoso hath this world's good, and seeth his brother have need, and shutteth up his bowels of compassion from him, how dwelleth the love of God in him? My little children, let us not love in word, neither in tongue; but in deed and in truth. (1 John 3:16–18)

Chapter 8

How to Forgive Men Their Trespasses

as We Forgive

And forgive us our debts, as we forgive our
debtors. And lead us not into temptation,
but deliver us from evil: For thine is the
kingdom, and the power, and the glory,
for ever. Amen. For if ye forgive men their
trespasses, your heavenly Father will also
forgive you: But if ye forgive not men their
trespasses, neither will your Father forgive
your trespasses. (Matt. 6:12)

Forgiveness is such a powerful tool. It can destroy a fortress,
uproot a mighty tree and set captives that have been held
in an emotional prison for years free in an instant.

When the disciples of Jesus asked Him to teach them how
to pray, forgiveness was a key factor in the lesson. The

lesson He gave about prayer taught us to pray, "Forgive us ... as we forgive." It was the lesson He continued to expound on after saying amen, and He told us God will treat us in forgiveness *as* we treat one another.

As a Grain of Mustard Seed

> And the Lord said, If ye had faith as a grain of mustard seed, ye might say unto this sycamine tree, Be thou plucked up by the root, and be thou planted in the sea; and it should obey you. (Luke 17:6)

In this discourse about "faith as a grain of mustard seed," we should pay attention to the context of the story and realize this discourse has very little to do with faith and everything to do with forgiveness (ref. Luke 17:1–5).

Jesus promised we would be offended by each other and instructed us to put no limits on how often we forgive each other. As soon as Jesus removed the right for us to carry an offence against someone else, the disciples asked Him to increase their faith. We are all very well aware of how it feels to be the offended one, and none of us are ready, in our natural man, to hand out forgiveness on a golden platter. It is much easier to desire that our offender gets their "just dues" because none of us deserve to be the offended one ... right?

Notice Jesus said "faith as" a grain of mustard seed. He did not say the size of a mustard seed. Forgiveness may take a season of time to grow just like a mustard seed takes a season of time to grow. However, we are required to sow the seeds of forgiveness within our souls by desiring to be "one with God and one with each other," even if it costs us a little humility in the process.

Once the seed is planted, (sown) within the fertile ground of our hearts' desire to be one with God, we can tend it with the water of God's Word and fertilize it with our love, mercy, and faith while we watch it grow into the mighty force of faith God has promised it could be. After all, we have freely received these gifts from God; we should be willing to freely give them to each other.

Miracles of healing are signs to the lost world that verify the Word of God to be true. The greatest miracle we can perform is the miracle of forgiving someone who has offended us or failed us or failed our Lord (ref. Matt. 10:8).

This is not some supernatural event; this is our duty! We are family, and we all have one Father. We are all guilty, and instead of quarreling with one another, we have reason to fall out with ourselves. We have all offended God and pray to be forgiven; therefore, we should all be ready to forgive one another.

When the world sees the church walking in this kind of faith, the world will want what (who) we possess: Jesus.

Chapter 9

Keep Your Eyes on the Prize

Press On

I press toward the mark for the prize of
the high calling of God in Christ Jesus.
(Phil. 3:14)

I want to address the hurting, wounded soldiers of the
cross. Regardless of the reason you are wounded—self-
afflicted or afflicted by another—your goal in life as
defined by the Lord has never changed. The Lord is still
coming, and you are still responsible to be ready as well as
help ready others for the day of His return.

You may have laid your weapons of warfare down or you
may have become so hurt and discouraged that you never
want to try again, but that does not change the fact that
God has called you into His service. The opposition was
more than you could bear, but you are still His soldier.
God did not make a mistake when He handpicked you,

appointed you, and called you into His service, and you did not misunderstand His call on your life.

To press toward denotes a heavy pursuit against intense opposition. If you expected the enemy of our souls to just lay down and not attempt to destroy you or your calling, you were sadly mistaken. The mark is the prize of the high calling of God, and you are already called.

Your focus may have become blurred, your heart may have lost its vigor, and your cross may have become heavier than you thought you could carry. But it is time to repent, stand back up, brush your spiritual self off, reenter the battle of the Lord, and keep on pressing.

You are risen with Christ; now seek the things that are above and set your affection on the things of Christ. When He called you, you became dead to the things of the earth, and your life has been hidden with Christ inside of God. It no longer matters that friends, family, churches, spouses, children, yourself, or anyone else has wounded you. The Lord is drawing near, and time is drawing short. What price is too high for you to pay?

Repent and be restored. If others continue to reject you, that is their problem, not yours.

> If ye then be risen with Christ, seek those
> things which are above, where Christ sitteth

on the right hand of God. Set your affection on things above, not on things on the earth. For ye are dead, and your life is hid with Christ in God. (Col. 3:1–3)

Be ye also patient; stablish your hearts: for the coming of the Lord draweth nigh. (James 5:8)

Perseverance

Confirming the souls of the disciples, and exhorting them to continue in the faith, and that we must through much tribulation enter into the kingdom of God. (Acts 14:22)

Sometimes we have added plenty of our own problems to our already promised "much tribulation" through poor choices in our Christian walk. But God is still in control of everything we can toss into the salad bowl of life. He will faithfully work everything out for our good and His divine purpose (ref. Rom. 8:28). We need to just keep going. To borrow a line from the animated film *Finding Nemo*, we need to "just keep swimming, just keep swimming …"

Never Give Up

Many years ago, British Prime Minister Winston Churchill was invited to speak at the graduation exercises of a prestigious private school. He was introduced to the students as one of the greatest statesmen of this century— the man who had managed to keep his nation united and fighting through the darkest days of World War II. He was furthermore described as one of the greatest orators of the modern era. The students were told that because they were about to hear, no doubt, a brilliant speech on the subject of character, they might want to take notes. As students fumbled for pencils and paper, Churchill grasped the edge of the lectern, stared intensely at his audience, and began: "I have only three truths to impart to you today on the subject of that virtue which makes a man. Let me begin by saying: *Never give up.* Let me continue by saying: *Never, never give up!* And in conclusion, I say to you: *Never, never, never give up!*" And with that Churchill sat down.

At the lowest point in King David's life when he was least likely to be king, he lost family, friends, and kingdom, and he wrote Psalm 23. He cried out, "I will fear no evil; for thou art with me; the rod and thy staff they comfort me. Thou preparest a table before me in presence of mine enemies ..." He stood with God, found his strength in the Lord, and passed his test. As a result, shortly after, David was recognized as the king of Israel and took his throne.

David was being prepared to run the great nation of God's people. God Himself was developing David's character. He was guilty of sin, yet he was not forsaken by the King of Kings. He persevered and won.

Job, who was an upright man in the kingdom of God, was diseased, bankrupt, wounded, and close to death. He was discouraged by his wife, accused of sin, and forsaken by his friends, but through all of his troubles, he kept his eyes on the prize. Through all of Job's struggles he said, "Though he slay me yet will I trust Him." He persevered, and he won.

Peter fled from the side of Jesus when his own life and the life of our Lord were at stake. Within moments he denied ever being with the Lord or even knowing Him. With cursing on his lips, Peter fled from Jesus in the greatest shame a man can ever bring on himself. In the midst of his shame and with great tears, he repented of his terrible failure and within a few days was restored by Jesus Himself. It is recorded that Peter failed at least one other time during his ministry on the earth but he "just kept going" (ref. Gal. 2:11–14). Peter persevered, and he won.

God has given us the victory through the finished work of our Lord Jesus Christ. We are simply required to be steadfast, unmovable, and abounding in our work for the Lord. It is time to run to the battle and get back on the firing line.

> But thanks *be* to God, which giveth us the victory through our Lord Jesus Christ. Therefore, my beloved brethren, be ye

stedfast, unmoveable, always abounding in the work of the Lord, forasmuch as ye know that your labour is not in vain in the Lord. (1 Cor. 15:57–58)

Chapter 10

Watch Who You Leave Behind

Spouse Killers in the Ministry

Some of the most overlooked and brutally wounded warriors in the church today are the pastors' wives. They are sitting on the sidelines wounded and bleeding and all too often go unnoticed.

Charles Stone, author of *Five Ministry Killers and How to Defeat Them*, quotes Ruthe White as saying, "The pastor's wife is the only woman I know who is asked to work full time without pay on her husband's job, in a role no one has yet defined."

(quoted from http://www.sermoncentral.com/pastors-preaching-articles/charles-stone-spouse-killers-in-the-ministry-754.asp)

One day my wife, the love of my life, Brenda, wrote about her difficulties when she was attempting to be the Proverbs 31 wife, only to find herself as a wounded warrior, bleeding and all but unnoticed on the battlefield of ministry.

When I read her story, my heart broke. I realized my expectations and her understandings were vastly different.

The results were devastating, and her wounds were deep. I needed to refocus on the prize, and this time, I would make sure to view it from four eyes instead of two eyes. From this day on, we would press on and persevere as one person in two bodies instead of two people just trying to make it in ministry.

Brenda's Story

Brenda Shackelford
March 1, 2012
Wounded Warrior or P31 Woman?

As I consider who I've been and who I've become, many things come to my mind. Who I've been is someone who has been seeking the Lord for many years, just wanting to build that intimate relationship with the Master of the universe. Who I've become is one who has engaged in that journey and doesn't have a clue as how she was to proceed. I've sought to become that virtuous woman, making mistakes along the way, but who I am now is a wounded warrior needing to retreat and regroup, going back, so to speak. As someone once told me, sometimes we have to go back before we can go forward.

When I consider my approach to this ministry, I see myself trying to become as the P31 woman. She did the things she felt were necessary to make her family strong and prosperous and independent. All that she engaged in was done with all her might. One might say she took ownership in her endeavors; she embraced them with all she was.

It has been said many times if one has no ownership in something or does not embrace the vision and its worth then it is not done with a spirit of excellence. We see the P31 woman as one who did things with a spirit of excellence. Her ability to make decisions was considered to be done well. Why? Because she was a woman who feared God. It doesn't ever tell of any failures in her life, only her success as a woman, a wife, a mother, and one who feared God.

Oh, to be that perfect P31. I know I will not probably ever be the woman she was although my heart and soul have strived to enter into the journey. I want strength and honor to be my clothing, my husband to be known in the gates and sit among the elders, my children to call me blessed, one who can make a decision to buy a field, plant it, bring in the harvest, and move onto the next thing, knowing what I have done is well because I have put my confidence in my heavenly Father.

She is not an idle woman. She is always looking for the next thing to be done. Why? So her husband is respected in the city gates and her family is taken care of well. She speaks with wisdom and kindness. Why? Because she is a woman who fears God, seeking after His perfect will for her life and the lives of her family and others. I can see by the way she clothes her family she's not afraid of hard work. She wants them to look their best but isn't worried if they get dirty. She knows they also walk in the favor of God, for she is a woman who fears God, taking care to demonstrate in all that she does is His character. She is diligent to the end as we see her beauty is fading, yet she still fears God, knowing it's not what's on the outside that matters but what is on the inside (the heart) that God sees and considers.

We see her work is worthy to be praised even among the city gates. She has a strong fortitude and a faith that will move mountains. Oh, who can find one so noble to stand by their side to be called wife, mom, and/or friend? All that we do as women is ministry, whether it be wife, mother, worker, or friend, we must do it and consider it as unto the *Lord*. How have I fared in this arena? My failures are great, to be sure … but as I consider where I've been and where I'm going, my heart is to continue the journey to the best of my ability as unto the *Lord*.

Will I fail again? I'm sure I will, but God gives me grace for the journey and strength for the day. Today I'm a wounded warrior and in need of the healing of the great Physician and the balm of Gilead to be applied, for the wounds are deep and many. But I know You are able, and so I cry out, "I'm Yours. Put me on your lap, Daddy. Hold me. Let me know *all* will be well soon so I might continue my journey to become that perfected P31."

March 2, 2012

As I continue to consider you, P31 woman, I have questions in my heart. When you were considering all the things you were doing, where was your husband? Were you beside him in his visions for his family or moving in your own agenda? Was it an unspoken expectation, or was it written or spoken? Did you just know what to do and how to do it? Did your husband agree with what you did and how you embraced the problem for the day? Did you have disagreements for the efforts you made in caring for your family? How did your husband respond to what appears to me to be a woman with her own mind—although it be the mind of Christ? Were you and he so connected within the Spirit of God that things just worked together like a well-oiled machine?

See, I'm stuck ... I have embraced every vision my husband has had since we've married. There were times when I didn't understand or even know exactly how I was to proceed, but I embraced it to the best of my ability. I proceeded with what I hoped was a spirit of excellence and decently and in order. Now I know I have failed many times just for the lack of spiritual knowledge, sometimes not being as learned as he, but that was to be expected. I was in training, right?

Did you P31 go through training? Oh, and yes sometimes I was slap wore out and overwhelmed, but I continued the journey. After all, my entire goal is to become a P31. When others left, I stayed and picked up what I would consider the right thing to do to walk beside my husband in his visions, only to find now that what he actually saw was me taking ownership of everything. Really? So I guess I have failed to understand how I was to proceed in all those visions …

Okay, maybe I didn't fully embrace Africa to level he wanted me to, but I did go. I guess at this point I'm just too tired to consider anything. So now what is his vision, and what part am I to do? Honestly, at this point I have nothing in it. I am too unsure to do anything or be anything. After all, according to my husband I'm in rebellion, and the way of a transgressor is rough. That's why I'm having such a hard time. So I'm releasing it *all*— no need to continue to embrace it or take any ownership in it. I'll finish the HH today, and I'm done. I'll go through the motions, but my hands are off. I'm at a loss of where to go from here. I don't want to be hurt or abused any longer. So Holy Spirit, without a revelation from You and a filling, I got nothing.

Your Spouse Is First

Wow, I was now facing another challenge of a lifetime. While reaching for strength and courage to continue in ministry, I had just discovered I was guilty of leaving my wife behind. It was time for me to redirect my heart toward my number-one ministry: my wife.

Called by God to be busy in Africa, helping rebuild a war-torn country, and needing to meet the needs of my own flesh and bone (Brenda), I was in a quandary. I could not see how it would be possible to follow God's call and stay in the United States at the same time. For eleven years she stood by my side, not always agreeing with or understanding me but always by my side. I now saw her hurting, wounded, and bleeding on the battlefield of ministry. I did not dare to move in either direction. I had to stand still, very still, and hear from God.

The Lord instructed me to meet Brenda's needs first, even if it meant I could not answer His call. It is impossible to explain my confusion at that time. My desire to make sure my wife, a great warrior of the Lord, was made whole before I entered into any additional ministry had to be my focus. When she saw me put her on top of my list, before any other ministry, she began to be restored. The Lord was speaking to her, and she was able to hear Him clearly. We entered into the mission field as *one* being, and the Lord has once again proven His faithfulness.

Chapter 11

Run to the Battle

Do You Want To Be Healed?

After this there was a feast of the Jews; and Jesus went up to Jerusalem. Now there is at Jerusalem by the sheep market a pool, which is called in the Hebrew tongue Bethesda, having five porches. In these lay a great multitude of impotent folk, of blind, halt, withered, waiting for the moving of the water. For an angel went down at a certain season into the pool, and troubled the water: whosoever then first after the troubling of the water stepped in was made whole of whatsoever disease he had. And a certain man was there, which had an infirmity thirty and eight years. When Jesus saw him lie, and knew that he had been now a long time in that case, he saith unto him, Wilt thou be made whole? The impotent man answered him, Sir, I have no man, when the water is troubled, to put me into the pool: but while I am coming, another steppeth down before me. Jesus saith unto him, Rise, take up thy bed, and walk. And immediately the man was made whole, and took up his bed, and walked: and on the same day was the sabbath. (John 5:1–9)

When Jesus sees us crippled by problems, crippled by circumstance, and crippled by sin, He says to us, "Do you want to get well?" Sometimes the answer lies within our own selves; do we really want it? Or do we want to continue to find excuses, blame others, blame circumstances, blame heredity, and blame anything except ourselves?

We often we hold on to tightly to the things that paralyze us spiritually. Jesus can heal us of those things, but when He does, we will be left without excuse for our lives and the choices we make. We will no longer be able to cry, "My life isn't my fault; others are to blame."

The Enemy will tell you it is easier to hold on to the hurt, but he has always been a liar and will only lie every time. Do you want Jesus to heal the parts of your life where you have been damaged? Or would you rather hang on to bitterness, wallow in your hurt and betrayal, and just try to lick your wounds?

To the wounded who has suffered the rejection of the church, the issue or problem is on *both* sides, not just the accuser or condemner's side. Put away the excuses and take authority over your decisions and circumstances. Stand up and be a man or woman of God. Take your position as a child of the Most High God. To be able to go forward, you must respond correctly to the call of God, and you know He is calling you right now! Do you want to be healed? It is just like this man in John 5 who wasn't healed until he took action. As soon as he took action, nothing and no one could stop him. Pick up whatever your mat is and walk! Your healing, your restoration, your life, and the lives of others depend on it. It is time for you to run to the battle and reengage in the ministry God has called you to.

The Battle Called Life

There is a battle, and the battle is real. Many men and women have fallen while engaged in this battle called life, and they are lying wounded and bleeding in the highways and the byways near the church. They have fallen among the thieves, been stripped of their raiment, and been left for dead by the church. The religious pass by them, look down upon them, and decide these fallen had their chance, and now the righteous religious are too busy remaining righteous and religious to mess with the fallen. *But God* is not finished with the dry bones. He is preparing His prophets in the land to prophesy life back into these fallen men and women on His battlefield called life.

What kind of army will come forth when God breathes into the nostrils of the fallen again? What kind of force will they be against the Enemy of our souls when they are restored and regain their hope?

These injured know how it feels to be disappointed or be a disappointment to others. These injured know how it feels to be a failure while others watched and judged them in their failures. These injured understand the power of an offense either given or received. These injured have an insight about fear hidden deep within the heart while they attempt to climb out of their despair. Once people experience a fall from right standing, they have a pure understanding of the pains, rejections, wounds, and host of additional emotions involved in such a fall. Upon restoration, this same army will be prepared to minister to others who find themselves in debasing situations and can offer hope to the hopeless and a hand up to those who may not even want one.

If you are still breathing, God is not finished with you yet. If you need someone to help you, God will send them to you. If you need courage, just remember the cross. *All* of your sins were paid for, and all of your guilt was taken away when Jesus *finished* the work.

"Can These Bones Live Again?"

I know a secret many in the church have forgotten. Nothing is done by our own might (strength), and nothing is done by power (a man's authority), but if it is going to happen, it happens by God's Spirit alone. So many have forgotten the work they are doing is only being accomplished through the Spirit of God and *not* the one who is working a righteous work. The Holy Spirit of God is interested in all souls, and He never loses connection with the souls He once cleaned up because He is faithfully married to them. God remains faithful even when we don't.

We must be careful not to think too highly of ourselves. In fact the Lord called us to be branches of Him who is the vine. When we know we are the branches, we will know our only purpose is to live for the glory of God while doing His work and bring forth fruit to the glory of His name. The Vine bears us, nourishes us, supplies us, and causes us to bring forth fruit that looks like it came from Jesus, who is the Root and who did not come to condemn the world.

It is high time for the unfallen church to repent of their arrogance, humble themselves, begin to pray as a branch of the True Vine, seek the same thing the True Vine seeks, begin to prophesy life back into the fallen church by the Spirit of God, and say to them, "The Lord will cause His Spirit, His breath, who He is, to enter into you, and you shall live and know He alone is God!"

The shame carried by the fallen church is enough! We can add to it by repetitive bashing, rejecting, and otherwise continued efforts to keep the fallen out of the race, or we can encourage the fallen to release their shame unto the Lord because He already took our shame on the cross.

Then prepare for the greatest revival America has ever seen.

The Mirror Is a Great Tool

When we weigh our lives against another, we can always find ourselves "good enough to cast a stone." But when we weigh our hearts against the holiness of God we discover ourselves just as guilty as the one we are so willing trying to stone to death.

Oh the judges that abound when the life of another is being weighed. Oh the tragedy that would become the life of the very judge who has abounded in the weighing of another when the judges heart and life becomes that which is being weighed. Oh how easy and convenient it becomes to shine the light of failure upon one who is in the eye of the public. Oh how inconvenient and difficult the abounding judges would suffer if they were to become the ones whose hearts were to be judged in the public eye. Oh how good it feels to show the failures and faults of an opponent, especially when their sins have so openly been revealed. Oh how bad it would feel if the secret failures and faults of the abounding judges were to be openly revealed.

> But I say unto you, That whosoever looketh on a woman to lust after her hath committed adultery with her already in his heart. (Matt. 5:28 KJV)

Oh the sins of the people of God who so excitedly kill their own with the stones of judgment. One would be wise to look in the mirror and reflect upon his hidden sins before picking up another rock and casting it so freely at one whose sins have been openly seen. The judgment of the abounding judges will also be without mercy when they have shown no mercy.

> For whosoever shall keep the whole law, and yet offend in one point, he is guilty of all. For he that said, Do not commit adultery, said also, Do not kill. Now if thou commit no adultery, yet if thou kill, thou art become a transgressor of the law. So speak ye, and so do, as they that shall be judged by the law of liberty. For he shall have judgment without mercy, that hath shewed no mercy; and mercy rejoiceth against judgment. (James 2:10–10 KJV)

Where He Leads Me and Guides Me, He Always Provides for Me

The Spirit of the Lord is sending His prophets through the land, calling out to His wounded army to heal them, restore them, and present them to the world for an end-times revival. Our Enemy has marked them off of his radar as dried up, hopeless, and finished. But God will breathe His restoring Spirit upon them again, and they will stand as a Mighty army for the Lord.

He led Israel to the Red Sea so He could split the sea. He led them to poisoned water so He could heal the waters. He led them to dry places so He could bring water from the rock. He led them to the wilderness where there was no food so He could feed them heaven's manna. He led thousands of men, women, and children to a place of hunger and exhaustion so He could feed them with a few pieces of bread and fish while they sat down and rested. He led Martha and Mary to the tomb of their brother Lazarus so he could raise a four-day-old dead man, and He will lead this great army of wounded soldiers of the cross to their final battle and total victory so we will all know the Lord alone has done the work.

Like the boy Joseph, you may have been hidden for a season, but even in your weakness, sin, and distress, the Lord has preserved you for this final hour (ref. Joseph's story from Gen. 39–45, esp. Gen. 45:7–8). He has given us a few of His names that contain promises of who He is and assured us of victory though His name.

He Said:

I am God Almighty.
I am Alpha and Omega.
I am the first and the last.
I am He that liveth and was dead.
I am the resurrection, and the life.
I am alive forevermore.
I am holy.
I am merciful.
I am gracious.

I am for you.

I am married unto you.

I am the good shepherd.

I am He who searcheth the reins and hearts.

I am He who comforteth you.

I am the LORD who healeth thee.

I am meek and lowly in heart.

I am the LORD who doth sanctify you.

I am the bread of life.

I am the door.

I am the light of the world.

I am the LORD who hallows you.

I am thy exceeding great reward.

I am thy salvation.

I am thy Savior.

I am thy shield.

I am the God of Abraham, and the God of Isaac, and the God of Jacob.

I am with you always.

Then He Told Us Who We Are:

We are the Lord's.

We are His offspring and loved of God.

We are buried with Him by baptism into death.

We are made one with God and made perfect in oneness.

We are more than conquerors through Him who loved us.

We are freed from sin and placed in grace.

We are saved by hope.

We are bought with a price.

We are washed, sanctified, and justified.

We are made the righteousness of God in Him.

We are enriched by Him in everything.

We are heirs of God and joint-heirs with Christ.

We are the children of God.

We are the temple of God.

We are laborers together with God.

We are God's husbandry, God's building.

We are the body of Christ and members in particular.

We are a sweet savor of Christ.

We are ambassadors of Christ.

We are the temple of the living God.

We are His workmanship, created in Christ Jesus.

We are fellow-citizens with the saints and the household of God.

We are members one of another.

We are sealed by the Holy Spirit of God.

We are light in the Lord.

We are holy and without blemish.

We are a glorious church.

We are members of His body, His flesh, and His bones.

We are the circumcision and in covenant with God.

We are complete in Him.

We are sanctified through the offering of His body.

We are in Him who is true.

We are dead to ourselves and risen with *Him* through the faith.

We are Christ's and made partakers of Christ.

We are all the children of light.

We are a chosen generation, a royal priesthood, and a holy nation.

We are a peculiar people.

We *are* now the people of God.

We are the children of the day.

We are the salt of the earth.

We are the light of the world.

We are of more value than many sparrows.

We are clean through the Word.

We are His friends.

We are the branches.

We are blessed in the city and blessed in the field.

We are blessed coming in and blessed going out.

We are blessed in everything we do and everything we own.

We are His people.

We are without spot, wrinkle, or any such thing.

And our life is hid with Christ in God.

Our old man is crucified with *Him, and* we shall be *in the likeness* of *His* resurrection because the Spirit of God dwells in us and God dwells in us and God walks in us.

We now have obtained mercy, we have the glory of Christ, and in Him we live, move, and have our being.

Conclusion

The hand of the LORD was upon me, and carried me out in the spirit of the LORD, and set me down in the midst of the valley which was full of bones, And caused me to pass by them round about: and, behold, there were very many in the open valley; and, lo, they were very dry. And he said unto me, Son of man, can these bones live? And I answered, O Lord GOD, thou knowest. Again he said unto me, Prophesy upon these bones, and say unto them, O ye dry bones, hear the word of the LORD. Thus saith the Lord GOD unto these bones; Behold, I will cause breath to enter into you, and ye shall live: And I will lay sinews upon you, and will bring up flesh upon you, and cover you with skin, and put breath in you, and ye shall live; and ye shall know that I am the LORD. So I prophesied as I was commanded: and as I prophesied, there was a noise, and behold a shaking, and the bones came together, bone to his bone. And when

I beheld, lo, the sinews and the flesh came up upon them, and the skin covered them above: but there was no breath in them. Then said he unto me, Prophesy unto the wind, prophesy, son of man, and say to the wind, Thus saith the Lord GOD; Come from the four winds, O breath, and breathe upon these slain, that they may live. So I prophesied as he commanded me, and the breath came into them, and they lived, and stood up upon their feet, an exceeding great army. Then he said unto me, Son of man, these bones are the whole house of Israel: behold, they say, Our bones are dried, and our hope is lost: we are cut off for our parts. Therefore prophesy and say unto them, Thus saith the Lord GOD; Behold, O my people, I will open your graves, and cause you to come up out of your graves, and bring you into the land of Israel. And ye shall know that I am the LORD, when I have opened your graves, O my people, and brought you up out of your graves, And shall put my spirit in you, and ye shall live, and I shall place you in your own land: then shall ye know that I the LORD have spoken it, and performed it, saith the LORD. (Ezek. 37:1–14)

I will end this book at the same place I started. I asked the question, "Can these bones live again?" But I would like to draw your attention to the person who is really asking this question. The Lord of glory Himself is asking His prophet if these bones can live again, and I believe He would ask all of His children the very same question today.

To all of us who have fallen or failed and to all of the righteous religious who have written church laws and bylaws and created doctrines preventing divorced men and women from ever ministering again, "Can these bones *ever* live again?" Can they *ever* be good enough to stand in your pulpits or serve in your public offices again?

I dare to challenge every one of *us* to consider the answer of the prophet of God, "O Lord *God, only You know!*" I dare challenge the condemners to look closely into their own lives, their own hidden sins, and their own beams in their own eyes and then answer the question, "Can—*these*—bones—live—*again?*"

If the Lord has the audacity to call these fallen soldiers of His cross to finish the work He has appointed them to do, even before the foundation of the earth, who dares to stand in the way? Who dares to decide their fate to be less than God's call on their lives? Who dares to make an oath or a law saying these men and women of God have no right to preach, teach, or otherwise minister God's Word and share

God's ways to a lost and dying world? Who dares to judge them as humans of poor character because of their failures?

I dare to challenge the church to see the character of the fallen who are willing to repent and get back up and keep on going as great. They have great character because of their willingness to face adversity coming from their own spiritual family. This family is willing to take in strangers and promote them to leadership all the while killing the fallen soldiers of the same cross they so freely offer the lost and dying world.

God will see the returning soldiers as His "exceedingly great army." God sees them as part of "the whole house of Israel." God sees them as a part of His body, and He is not willing to have a part of His body left out. He is coming for a whole bride, not a crippled one. God sees their character as worthwhile to entrust His gospel message to.

God will finish what He has started. These bones will have His breath in them once again, and *they will be the revival the church is praying for!*

Amen

About the Author

Forty years ago, Don Shackelford received the Lord Jesus Christ as his personal Lord and Savior. Seven years later, Don co-founded his first church serving as the associate pastor.

In 1998 Don became the senior pastor of a local community church in South Carolina. During his fifteen-year tenure as the senior pastor, he founded a sixty-five-child childcare facility, a Sunday morning and Sunday evening Christian church service for both men and women in the county jail, a drug and alcohol rehab housing facility for men coming out of jail, a private Christian school for children from preschool to twelfth grade, and a safe house for abused women and children, and he has supported various missions in two different countries in Africa.

Today Don and his wife, Brenda, are missionaries in Africa concentrating on the rebuilding of the war-torn nation of Sierra Leone, bringing new industries to that country, building schools, churches, and agriculture opportunities, and supporting the training of new pastors being sent out to the provinces. They also continue the support of building a world-class orphanage in Mozambique, SE Africa.

Don can be reached at:
www.lcmrm.com
lalpd@yahoo.com
843-817-8878